STARTER
WORKBOOK
with Digital Pack
CEFR
A1

AMERICAN TH!NK

SECOND EDITION

Herbert Puchta,
Jeff Stranks &
Peter Lewis-Jones
with Vicki Anderson

CAMBRIDGE
UNIVERSITY PRESS

ACKNOWLEDGEMENTS

Author

The authors and publishers acknowledge the following sources of copyright material and are grateful for the permissions granted. While every effort has been made, it has not always been possible to identify the sources of all the material used, or to trace all copyright holders. If any omissions are brought to our notice, we will be happy to include the appropriate acknowledgements on reprinting and in the next update to the digital edition, as applicable.

Key: UW = Unit Welcome; U = Unit.

Photography

All the photographs are sourced from Getty Images.

UW: Westend61; David Crespo/Moment; Vostok/Moment; Elen11/iStock/Getty Images Plus; Prasit photo/Moment; Barcin/iStock/Getty Images Plus; WIN-Initiative/Stone; Vesnaandjic/E+; Tharakorn Arunothai/EyeEm; Vesna Jovanovic/EyeEm; Mint Images/Mint Images RF; Barry Wong/The Image Bank; Rainer Grosskopf/Photolibrary; Ng Sok Lian/EyeEm; hudiemm/E+; monkeybusinessimages/iStock/Getty Images Plus; Circle Creative Studio/iStock/Getty Images Plus; MmeEmil/E+; Siri Stafford/Photodisc; **U1:** Jonathan Kirn/The Image Bank; avdeev007/E+; filipefrazao/iStock/Getty Images Plus; LeoPatrizi/E+; Rifka Hayati/E+; Mike Kemp; AfricaImages/iStock/Getty Images Plus; Henrik5000/E+; prill/iStock/Getty Images Plus; Quality Sport Images/Getty Images Sport; Kelly Defina/Getty Images Sport; Sorapong Chaipanya/EyeEm; 10'000 Hours/DigitalVision; shaunl/iStock/Getty Images Plus; Thurtell/E+; Poligrafistka/DigitalVision Vectors; fstop123/E+; Kypros/Moment; Morsa Images/DigitalVision; FLMfotografia/Fernando Lobos Miralles/Moment Open; Compassionate Eye Foundation/DigitalVision; mtreasure/iStock/Getty Images Plus; Marcel Germain/Moment; luoman/E+; Yoshio Tomii/Photolibrary; **U2:** monkeybusinessimages/iStock/Getty Images Plus; FatCamera/E+; Westend61; Aditya Sethia/EyeEm; **U3:** Danielle Kiemel/Moment; MargaretW/iStock/Getty Images Plus; gerenme/iStock/Getty Images Plus; petrenkod/iStock/Getty Images Plus; Jason Finn/iStock/Getty Images Plus; LeeYiuTung/iStock/Getty Images Plus; medusaphotography/iStock/Getty Images Plus; anmbph/iStock/Getty Images Plus; RuthBlack/iStock/Getty Images Plus; Thomas Barwick/Stone; svetikd/E+; Hazmi Che Man/EyeEm; Obradovic/E+; John Slater/The Image Bank Unreleased; **U4:** Maskot; Image Source; Feifei Cui-Paoluzzo/Moment; Rafael Ben-Ari/The Image Bank; mindscanner/iStock/Getty Images Plus; violinconcertono3/iStock/Getty Images Plus; AlixKreil/iStock/Getty Images Plus; Violetta Potapova/EyeEm; Guerilla; Yellow Dog Productions/DigitalVision; akinshin/iStock/Getty Images Plus; fcafotodigital/E+; sanchesnet1/iStock/Getty Images Plus; scanrail/iStock/Getty Images Plus; Yevgen Romanenko/Moment; **U5:** Sol de Zuasnabar Brebbia/Moment; Thomas Barwick/Stone; **U6:** wagnerokasaki/E+; Indeed; Paul Vozdic/The Image Bank; Rick Gomez; SerhiiBobyk/iStock/Getty Images Plus; Westend61; Fuse/Corbis; Mint Images/Mint Images RF; triocean/iStock/Getty Images Plus; SolStock/E+; kate_sept2004/E+; Paul Bradbury/OJO Images; shapecharge/E+; Artem Varnitsin/EyeEm; Lane Oatey/Blue Jean Images; skynesher/E+; Wavebreakmedia/iStock/Getty Images Plus; **U7:** gazanfer/iStock/Getty Images Plus; JoyImage/iStock/Getty Images Plus; Bryn Lennon/Getty Images Sport; Junya Nishigawa - PARAPHOTO/Getty Images Sport; Fuse/Corbis; kyoshino/iStock/Getty Images Plus; **U8:** Inti St Clair; joingate/iStock/Getty Images Plus; Kim Grosz/EyeEm; **U9:** Emma Farrer/Moment; Science Photo Library; Floortje/E+; Byjeng/iStock/Getty Images Plus; Yothin Sanchai/EyeEm; Natthakan Jommanee/EyeEm; Nattawut Lakjit/EyeEm; bergamont/iStock/Getty Images Plus; eli_asenova/E+; ManuWe/E+; Creativeye99/E+; FotografiaBasica/iStock/Getty Images Plus; Getty Images/EyeEm; Marat Musabirov/iStock/Getty Images Plus; Hyrma/iStock/Getty Images Plus; Nirut Punshiri/EyeEm; LauriPatterson/E+; pamela_d_mcadams/iStock/Getty Images Plus; Simon Belcher; AnnaPustynnikova/iStock/Getty Images Plus; Nettiya Nithascharukul/EyeEm; Burcu Atalay Tankut/Moment; **U10:** Underwood Archives/Archive Photos; WPA Pool/Getty Images News; IMAGEMORE Co.,Ltd.; Sylvain Lefevre/Getty Images Entertainment; Print Collector/Hulton Archive; George Pachantouris/Moment; Jesse Grant/Getty Images Entertainment; Noam Galai/Getty Images Entertainment; Topical Press Agency/Hulton Archive; INDRANIL MUKHERJEE/AFP; UniversalImagesGroup/Universal Images Group; Universal History Archive/Universal Images Group; SDI Productions/E+; **U11:** izusek/E+; moodboard; MichaelJust/iStock/Getty Images Plus; Chris McNeill/500px Prime; Fernán Quetequitenloviajao/500Px Plus; by Simon Gakhar/Moment Open; CreativeNature_nl/iStock/Getty Images Plus; Mark Hamblin/Oxford Scientific; Andrea Edwards/EyeEm; Philartphace/E+; shuchun ke/500px/500PX Plus; Maria Jeffs/iStock/Getty Images Plus; Sergio Amiti/Moment; kickers/E+; Image Source; DEA PICTURE LIBRARY/De Agostini Picture Library; FierceAbin/E+; Richard Nowitz/DigitalVision; **U12:** Mike Kemp; Luis Franceschi/EyeEm; Steve Raymer/Corbis D;ocumentary; wsfurlan/E+; MicroStockHub/iStock/Getty Images Plus; simonbradfield/E+.

The following photographs are sourced from other sources/libraries.

U2: Courtesy of LBI Entertainment, LLC; **U10:** Mike Blenkinsop/Alamy Stock Photo.

Cover photography by Konstantin Tronin/Shutterstock; © Marco Bottigelli/Moment/Getty Images

Illustrations

UW: Ben Scruton; Adam Linley; Emma Nyari; **U1**: Ben Scruton; Martin Sanders; Mark Ruffle; **U2**: Dusan Lakicevic; emc design ltd; **U3**: Ben Scruton; Adam Linley; Mark Ruffle; Martin Sanders; **U4**: Martin Sanders; Adam Linley; Martin Sanders; Dusan Lakicevic; Mark Ruffle; **U5**: Dusan Lakicevic; Adam Linley; Mark Ruffle; **U6**: Emma Nyari; Ben Scruton; **U7**: Dusan Lakicevic; Ben Scruton; Adam Linley; Mark Ruffle; **U8**: Emma Nyari; **U9 & U10**: Adam Linley; **U11**: Mark Ruffle; **U12**: Dusan Lakicevic; Martin Sanders; Adam Linley.

The Vlog & Grammar Rap Video Stills: Silversun Media Group

Audio Production: CityVox, New York

CONTENTS

3

WELCOME

The alphabet

1 🔊 W.01 **Listen and write the names and the cities.**

Names

0 _B o b b y_
1 _ _ _ _ _
2 _ _ _ _ _ _
3 _ _ _ _ _
4 _ _ _ _ _ _ _ _
5 _ _ _ _ _ _

Cities

6 _ _ _ _ _
7 _ _ _ _ _ _ _
8 _ _ _ _ _ _ _ _
9 _ _ _ _ _ _ _ _
10 _ _ _ _ _ _
11 _ _ _ _ _ _ _ _

2 **Match to make the words.**

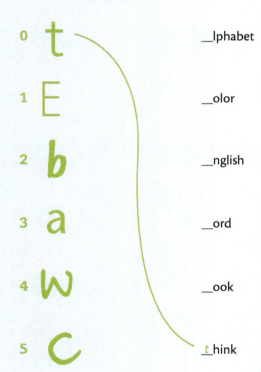

0 **t**   __lphabet

1 **E**   __olor

2 **b**   __nglish

3 **a**   __ord

4 **w**   __ook

5 **C**   _t_ hink

Colors

3 🔊 W.02 **Listen and write the colors. Then color the pictures in the correct color.**

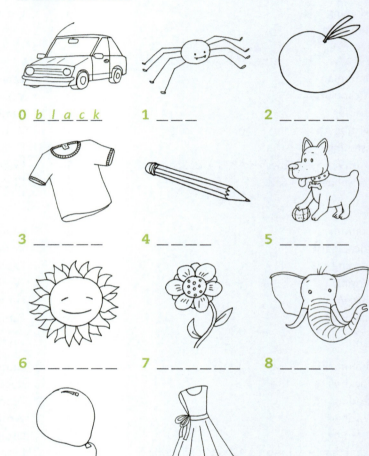

0 _b l a c k_   1 _ _ _ _   2 _ _ _ _ _ _

3 _ _ _ _ _ _   4 _ _ _ _ _   5 _ _ _ _ _

6 _ _ _ _ _ _ _   7 _ _ _ _ _ _ _   8 _ _ _ _ _

9 _ _ _ _ _ _ _   10 _ _ _ _ _

4 **Find ten more colors in the word search and color the squares in the correct color.**

b	l	a	c	k	u	y	d	e	r
e	g	r	e	e	n	e	e	e	b
n	o	y	d	w	x	l	g	u	a
w	w	a	o	e	k	l	n	l	c
o	h	r	r	k	n	o	a	b	k
r	i	g	n	e	i	w	r	e	y
b	t	i	g	k	p	u	o	l	i
p	e	p	e	l	p	r	u	p	g

International words

5 Put the letters in order to make words.

0 trapior
airport

1 sub

2 facé

3 -FiiW

4 rakp

5 ccores

6 rbumagerh

7 thole

8 iytc

9 openh

10 zizap

11 tranaruset

12 cinadswh

13 axit

14 si-Thtr

15 bleatt

6 🔊 W.03 Listen and put the words in order.

a ☐ hamburger
b ☐ airport
c ☐ phone
d ☐ pizza
e ☐ café
f ☐ park
g ☐ tablet
h ☑ *1* T-shirt
i ☐ hotel
j ☐ city

SUMMING UP

7 🔊 W.04 Listen and draw.

1	2	3

4	5	6

Articles: *a* and *an*

1 Circle the correct options.

0 *a* / *an* orange bus
1 *a* / *an* gray airport
2 *a* / *an* American TV
3 *a* / *an* white tablet
4 *a* / *an* English actor
5 *a* / *an* hamburger
6 *a* / *an* yellow taxi
7 *a* / *an* phone
8 *a* / *an* Italian car
9 *a* / *an* red bus

2 Write the words in the list in the correct columns. Then write five more words in each column.

actor | airport | apple | city
hamburger | hotel | orange | taxi

a	*an*
city	

The day

3 Look at the pictures and complete the phrases.

0 Good *m o r n i n g*
2 Good _ _ _ _ _ _ _

1 Good _ _ _ _ _ _ _ _ _
3 Good _ _ _ _ _ _ _ _ _

Saying *Hello* and *Goodbye*

4 Write the words in the list under the pictures.

Bye | Good afternoon
Good evening | Good morning
Good night | H̶e̶l̶l̶o̶ | Hi | See you

_____ *Hello.* _____   _____
_____ _____

_____ _____   _____
_____ _____

SUMMING UP

5 🔊 **W.05** **Put the conversations in order. Then listen and check.**

Conversation 1

☐ **Holly**   Good morning, Mr. Wood.

☐ **Holly**   I'm fine. And you?

☐ **Mr. Wood**   Hello, Holly. How are you?

☐ **Mr. Wood**   I'm great, thanks.

Conversation 2

☐ **Nick**   Yeah, have a good day.

☐ **Nick**   Bye, Jodie.

☐ **Jodie**   Bye, Nick. See you later.

Conversation 3

☐ **Alex**   I'm fine, thank you.

☐ **Alex**   Bye, Mrs. Young.

☐ **Alex**   Good afternoon, Mrs. Young.

☐ **Mrs. Young**   Good. I'll see you in class.

☐ **Mrs. Young**   Hello, Alex. How are you?

6 **Write short dialogues.**

Carmen   *Hello.*

Leo   _____

Jake   _____

Carmen   _____

Dora   _____

Dad   _____

Classroom objects

1 **Match the pictures with the words in the list. Write 1–10 in the boxes.**

> **1** book | **2** chair | **3** computer
> **4** desk | **5** door | **6** pen | **7** pencil
> **8** projector | **9** board | **10** window

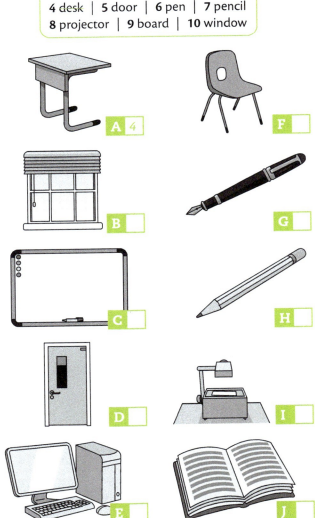

A 4   **F** ☐

B ☐   **G** ☐

C ☐   **H** ☐

D ☐   **I** ☐

E ☐   **J** ☐

2 **Use the letters from Exercise 1 to complete the crossword.**

E

B   F

G

H↓ I→

C→ J↓
b

o

D   o

k

Numbers 0–20

3 **Write the numbers.**

0	four	4	**11**	seven	___
1	eight	___	**12**	sixteen	___
2	twenty	___	**13**	eighteen	___
3	five	___	**14**	ten	___
4	twelve	___	**15**	fourteen	___
5	six	___	**16**	three	___
6	eleven	___	**17**	thirteen	___
7	one	___	**18**	seventeen	___
8	fifteen	___	**19**	two	___
9	nineteen	___	**20**	nine	___
10	zero	___			

Plural nouns

4 **How many do you see? Look, count, and write the plurals.**

> book | chair | child | computer | door | man
> pencil | pen | phone | window | woman

0	eight	men
1	three	___
2	seven	___
3	fifteen	___
4	eighteen	___
5	two	___
6	one	___
7	zero	___
8	twelve	___
9	four	___
10	six	___

Classroom language

5 **Circle the correct options.**

0 Close your books. / (What does this mean?)

4 Listen. / Look at the picture.

1 Raise your hand. / Close your books.

5 Work with a partner. / Raise your hand.

2 Listen. / That's right.

6 Open your books. / Look at the picture.

3 Work with a partner. / That's wrong.

SUMMING UP

6 🔊 **W.06** **Listen and check (✓) the sentences that you hear.**

1 There are three books. ☐

2 Open your books. ☐

3 There are 20 children in the class. ☐

4 What does this mean? ☐

5 There are two windows. ☐

6 Raise your hand. ☐

Numbers 20–100

1 Write the numbers.

0 seventy _____70_____

1 thirty _____

2 forty _____

3 ninety _____

4 a hundred _____

5 fifty _____

6 twenty _____

7 sixty _____

8 eighty _____

9 thirty-four _____

10 sixty-eight _____

11 twenty-one _____

12 ninety-nine _____

13 fifty-three _____

2 🔊 W.07 Listen and write the numbers.

0 _____thirty-four_____

a _____

b _____

c _____

d _____

e _____

f _____

g _____

h _____

i _____

j _____

k _____

Messages

3 🔊 W.08 Listen to the messages and (circle) the correct options.

Message 1

Message for Joe from David ⁰Jones / (James.)

His office is at number ¹6 / 7

²Thames / Temms Road.

The train station is ³Cue / Kew Bridge.

His phone number is ⁴202-686-7580 /

202-868-7580.

Message 2

Debbie's message from Claire Greene.

The party is at the ⁵Britannia / Breton Hotel.

The address of the hotel is ⁶44 / 34

South Street.

The bus number is ⁷15 / 16.

Her phone number is ⁸214-455-6445 /

214-563-4453.

SUMMING UP

4 🔊 W.09 Listen and complete the messages.

Message 1

Hi Daniel,

Message from Mr. ⁰_____Cleverly_____.

His address is ¹_____

King Street.

The bus to take is number ²_____.

His phone number is ³_____

676-7450.

Message 2

Hi Erica,

Message from Jane ⁴_____.

Her house number is ⁵_____

on Linton Road.

The name of the station is ⁶_____ City.

Her phone number is 415-780 ⁷_____.

1 ALL TOGETHER

Grammar rap!

▶02

GRAMMAR
Question words

→ SB p.14

1 ⭐☆☆ **Complete the sentences with the correct question words.**

0 ___*What*___ is your name?

1 _____ old are you?

2 _____ are you from?

3 _____ is your favorite athlete?

4 _____ is he / she your favorite athlete?

2 ⭐⭐⭐ **Write answers to the questions in Exercise 1 so they are true for you.**

0 *My name is ...* _____

1 _____

2 _____

3 _____

4 _____

PRONUNCIATION
/h/ or /w/ in question words
Go to page 118. 🎧

3 ⭐⭐☆ **Look at the pictures and circle the correct words.**

0 *He / She / It* is happy.

1 *We / You / I* are friends.

2 *They / We / You* are Brazilian.

3 *She / He / It* is eleven.

4 *I / She / We* am Sonia.

5 *We / They / You* are Mario.

6 *We / I / They* are sisters.

7 *I / It / You* is the Turkish flag.

to be

 SB p.15

4 ★☆☆ **Complete the table with the words in the list.**

am | are | are | are | is | is | is

0	I	*am*	Jon.
1	You		thirteen.
2	He		happy.
3	She		from Spain.
4	It		Indonesian.
5	We		sisters.
6	They		friends.

5 ★★☆ **Complete the sentences with the correct form of the verb *to be*. Use contracted forms.**

0 You*'re* Spanish.

1 I__ Mexican.

2 We__ Russian.

3 They__ Indonesian.

4 He__ American.

5 She__ Brazilian.

6 ★★☆ **Rewrite the sentences using contracted forms.**

0 It is a Japanese flag.
It's a Japanese flag

1 She is Sudanese.
_____

2 You are a good friend.
_____

3 They are British.
_____

4 We are from New York.
_____

5 I am Andres. What is your name?
_____

6 He is 12 today.
_____

GET IT RIGHT!

Subject–verb agreement with *be*

We use the form of *be* that agrees with the subject.

✓ *They are from Italy.*   ✗ *They is from Italy.*

Correct the sentences.

0 There are a beautiful beach.
There is a beautiful beach.

1 The classes is for two hours.
_____

2 It are cold today.
_____

3 Are the English player good?
_____

4 We's from Mexico.
_____

5 My favorite country are Japan.
_____

11

VOCABULARY
Countries and nationalities

→ SB p.14

1 ★☆☆ **Find 11 more countries in the word search. Then write the countries.**

N	H	I	S	O	C	I	X	E	M
I	B	R	A	Z	I	L	S	I	E
N	A	D	U	S	S	K	O	N	T
K	C	N	A	M	P	S	U	D	U
U	Y	E	I	F	A	L	T	O	R
E	M	Z	S	E	I	S	H	N	K
H	P	B	S	K	A	P	A	E	E
T	H	E	U	S	P	A	F	S	Y
A	C	V	R	W	K	I	R	I	J
E	J	A	P	A	N	N	I	A	Q
R	R	K	A	Y	H	B	C	N	M
E	C	U	A	D	O	R	A	L	D

0 ___Brazil___   6 _____
1 _____   7 _____
2 _____   8 _____
3 _____   9 _____
4 _____   10 _____
5 _____   11 _____

2 ★★☆ **Complete the words.**

0 Peter's from Cape Town. He's South Afric _an_ .

1 He's from Glasgow. He's Briti____ .

2 I'm from Mexico City. I'm Mexic____ .

3 Ella's from Chicago. She's Americ____ .

4 They're from Valencia. They're Span____ .

5 You're from Moscow. You're Russi____ .

6 My mom is from Rio de Janeiro.
She's Brazili____ .

7 Our teacher is from Java. He's Indones____ .

8 Haruki is from Tokyo. He's Japan____ .

9 They're from Istanbul. They're Turk____ .

10 My dad is from Khartoum. He's Sudan____ .

11 Ana and Luz are from Quito.
They're Ecuador____ .

Adjectives

→ SB p.17

3 ★☆☆ **Write the adjectives from the list under the pictures.**

> big | cheap | clean | dirty | expensive
> fast | new | old | slow | small

The car is …

0 ___big___   2 _____   4 _____
1 _____   3 _____

The car is …

5 _____   7 _____   9 _____
6 _____   8 _____

4 ★★☆ **Put the words in order to make sentences.**

0 book / English / My / new / is / .
My English book is new.

1 red / Her / is / pen / .
_____

2 is / house / old / Our / .
_____

3 fast / bikes / Their / are / .
_____

4 big / school / Our / is / .
_____

5 My / small / bedroom / is / .
_____

6 car / Her / expensive / is / .
_____

REFERENCE

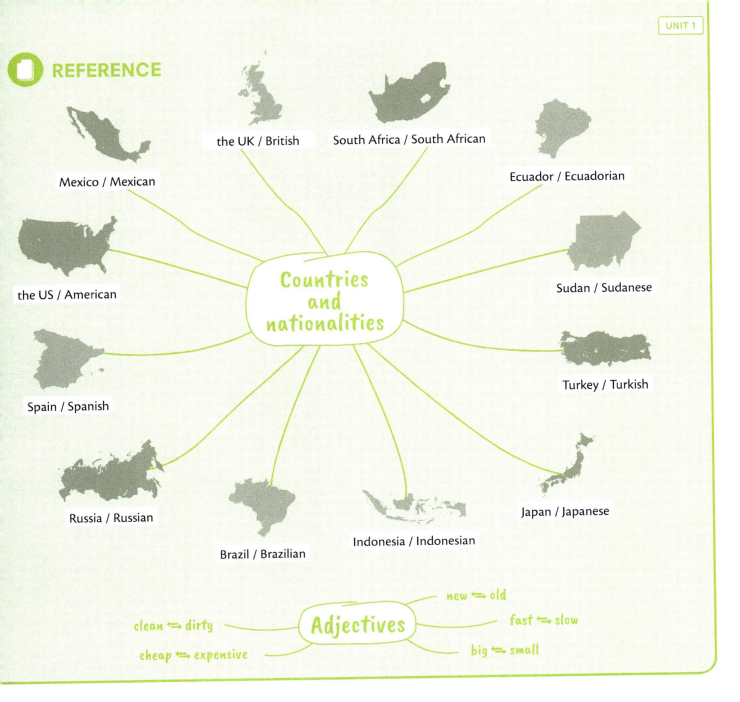

Countries and nationalities

Mexico / Mexican

the UK / British

South Africa / South African

Ecuador / Ecuadorian

the US / American

Sudan / Sudanese

Spain / Spanish

Turkey / Turkish

Russia / Russian

Brazil / Brazilian

Indonesia / Indonesian

Japan / Japanese

Adjectives

new ⇆ old

clean ⇆ dirty

cheap ⇆ expensive

fast ⇆ slow

big ⇆ small

VOCABULARY *EXTRA*

1 **Write an adjective from the list under each picture.**

hard | high | long | low | short | soft

0 _____short_____ 1 _____ 2 _____ 3 _____ 4 _____ 5 _____

2 **Put the adjectives from Exercise 1 in pairs with their opposites.**

_____ ⇆ _____

_____ ⇆ _____

_____ ⇆ _____

Hi, my name's Hugo. I'm Mexican. I'm from Acapulco. I'm 12 years old. My favorite athlete is Ricky Rubio. He's Spanish. He's a basketball player in the NBA. He's great.

 My name's Maddison. I'm ten years old. I'm Canadian, from Vancouver. My favorite athlete is Sofia Kenin. She's a tennis player. She's from the US. She's awesome!

 Hi, I'm Yusuf. I'm 13 years old. I'm Turkish. I'm from Ankara, the capital. My favorite athlete is Kylian Mbappé. He's a soccer player from Paris, France. He's an amazing player.

 Hi there! My name's Mia. I'm 12 years old. I'm South African, from the city of Cape Town. My favorite athlete is Adam Peaty. He's a swimmer from the UK. He's really fast.

 My name's Gabriella. I'm 11 years old. I'm British, from London. I think my favorite athlete is Dina Asher-Smith. She's a runner in the 100m and 200m races. She's also from London, and she's really fast!

📖 READING

1 Read the texts quickly. Where are they from? Match the names with the countries.

0 Hugo		**a** the UK
1 Maddison		**b** South Africa
2 Yusuf		**c** Mexico
3 Mia		**d** Turkey
4 Gabriella		**e** Canada

2 Read the texts again. Mark the sentences T (true) or F (false).

0 Hugo is from Mexico City. — F

1 Hugo's favorite athlete is a soccer player. ☐

2 Maddison is ten. ☐

3 Maddison's favorite athlete is a Canadian tennis player. ☐

4 Yusuf is from the capital of Turkey. ☐

5 Yusuf's favorite athlete is French. ☐

6 Mia is 11. ☐

7 Mia's favorite athlete is British. ☐

8 Gabriella's favorite athlete is a woman. ☐

9 Gabriella and Dina are from London. ☐

3 **CRITICAL THINKING** Now think about your favorite athlete and write.

1 What's his/her name?

_____

2 What sport does he/she do?

_____

3 Where is he/she from?

_____

4 Why is he/she your favorite athlete?

_____

DEVELOPING Writing

About me

1 INPUT **Read the questionnaire. Where is Maria from?**

New England
M u s i c   A c a d e m y

Be the best – Summer Music Camp on the East Coast!

Pop, rap, reggaeton, R&B, country – we can help you be the best!

We want to know all about you.

▶ What's your name?   Maria Garcia

▶ Where are you from?   Guadalajara, Mexico

▶ How old are you?   12

▶ What's your favorite music?   pop

▶ Who's your favorite singer?   Miley Cyrus

2 ANALYZE **Complete the text about Maria with the missing words.**

Hi, my name is ⁰_____Maria_____ .
I'm Mexican. I'm from ¹_____ .
I'm ²_____ years old. I love
a lot of music! My favorite music is
³_____ . It's great! I love rap
and reggaeton, too. My favorite singer
is ⁴_____ . She's a singer from
Tennessee, in the US. She's amazing!
Her father is a country singer.

3 PLAN **Complete the questionnaire about you.**

New England
M u s i c   A c a d e m y

Be the Best – Summer Music Camp on the East Coast!
Pop, rap, reggaeton, R&B, country – we can help you be the best!
We want to know all about you.

▶ What's your name? _____
▶ Where are you from? _____
▶ How old are you? _____
▶ What's your favorite music? _____
▶ Who's your favorite singer? _____

4 PRODUCE **Use your answers from Exercise 3 to complete a text about you. Use the text in Exercise 2 to help you.**

Hi, my name is _____ .
I'm _____ . I'm from
_____ . I'm
_____ old. My favorite
music is _____ . I love
_____ , too. My favorite
_____ . He's / She's
_____ . He's / She's
_____ !

✎ WRITING TIP: Checking

When you finish, always read your writing again. Check for mistakes.

• Do all the verbs agree with their subjects?

🎧 LISTENING

1 🔊 1.03 Listen to the conversation. Number the nationalities in the order you hear them. Write 1–5 in the boxes.

 **A** ☐

1 _____

 **B** ☐

2 _____

 **C** ☐

3 _____

 **D** ☐

4 _____

  **E** ☐

5 _____

2 🔊 1.03 Listen again and write the names under the photos in Exercise 1.

> Alice | Ben | Afia | Miguel | Santi

3 Circle the correct answers (A or B).

0 Afia is from …
  Ⓐ Sudan.   **B** Spain.
1 Santi is from …
  A Seville.   **B** Shanghai.
2 Ben is from …
  A Chile.   **B** Spain.
3 Alice is from …
  A the UK.   **B** Ecuador.
4 Miguel is from …
  A London.   **B** Quito.

DIALOGUE

4 Circle the correct answers (A, B, or C) to complete the conversation.

Boy Hi, what's your name?
Girl I'm **0** **A** 12.
              B Brazil.
              Ⓒ Alex.
Boy And where are you from?
Girl **1** **A** I'm Canadian.
              B I'm 11.
              C Sara.
Boy What city are you from?
Girl **2** **A** Japan.
              B Toronto.
              C Mexico.
Boy Toronto's a beautiful city.
Girl **3** **A** Yes, I am.
              B Yes, it is.
              C Yes, they are.
Boy Who's your favorite singer?
Girl **4** **A** Shawn Mendes.
              B Lionel Messi.
              C Yes.
Boy Why is he your favorite singer?
Girl **5** **A** No.
              B Yes.
              C Because he's so awesome.
Boy Nice to meet you, Alex.
Girl **6** **A** Yes.
              B No.
              C Nice to meet you, too.

PHRASES FOR FLUENCY   → SB p.18

5 Match the phrases (1–4) with their meanings (a–d).

1 How's it going?   **a** Goodbye.
2 See you later.   **b** How are you?
3 I know.   **c** Great.
4 That is so awesome!   **d** You're right.

6 Use the phrases 1–4 from Exercise 5 to complete the dialogues.

1 **A** Hi, David. _____
  B I'm fine, thanks.
2 **A** Bye, Tomas.
  B Bye, Lina. _____
3 **A** This is my new tablet.
  B _____
4 **A** Raheem's a great soccer player.
  B _____

SUM IT UP

1 Where do you see these things?

1
- A the US
- B the UK
- C Italy

3
- A Mexico
- B Brazil
- C China

2
- A the US
- B Australia
- C Russia

4
- A Japan
- B the US
- C Spain

2 Where do they say "hello" like this?

1 "How's it going?"
- A the US
- B Portugal
- C Colombia

2 "Buenos dias"
- A Argentina
- B Turkey
- C Australia

3 "Konnichiwa"
- A Russia
- B China
- C Japan

4 "Merhaba"
- A Russia
- B Turkey
- C Ecuador

3 Where are these capital cities?

1 Paris
- A Sudan
- B France
- C Italy

2 Pretoria
- A The UK
- B Mexico
- C South Africa

3 Ankara
- A Morocco
- B Turkey
- C Spain

4 Brasilia
- A France
- B Russia
- C Brazil

4 Who is from ...

1 Brazil?
- A Neymar
- B Kylian Mbappé
- C Ed Sheeran

2 the UK?
- A Taylor Swift
- B Simone Biles
- C Lewis Hamilton

3 Spain?
- A Lady Gaga
- B Ricky Rubio
- C Post Malone

4 the US?
- A Gigi Hadid
- B Harry Kane
- C Shawn Mendes

2 I'M EXCITED

GRAMMAR

to be (negative, singular, and plural) →→ SB p.22

1 ★☆☆ **Circle** the correct form of *to be*.

0 Joao (is)/ am happy today. It ('s)/ 're his birthday.
1 We *am / are* excited. We *'s / 're* on vacation.
2 It *'s / 'm* late. I *'s / 'm* tired.
3 Elena and Ana *is / are* happy. They *is / are* on the tennis team.
4 You *are / is* angry.
5 It *is / are* hot here.

2 ★★☆ **Complete the sentences with the correct negative form of *to be*.**

0 I ____'m not____ tired. I'm worried.
1 Paulo _____ happy. He's bored.
2 Zehra and Jane _____ worried. They're excited.
3 We _____ angry with you. We're worried about you, that's all.
4 Marina _____ happy at her new school. Her new classmates _____ very friendly.
5 It _____ hot in here. It's cold. Close the window.
6 I _____ hungry. I'm thirsty.

to be (questions and short answers) →→ SB p.23

3 ★★☆ **Circle** the correct form of *to be*.

1 A *Is /* (Are) Julia and Matt with you?
  B No, they *isn't / aren't*.
2 A *Am / Is* I on your team?
  B Yes, you *is / are*.
3 A *Am / Are* you at the beach now?
  B No, we *isn't / aren't*.
4 A *Is / Are* Nico at home?
  B No, he *isn't / aren't*.
5 A *Is / Are* Erin at school today?
  B Yes, she *is / are*.
6 A *Am / Are* you American?
  B No, I *'m not / aren't*.

4 ★★☆ **Write the questions. Then write answers so they are true for you.**

0 your name / Maria?
  Is your name Maria?   *No, it isn't.*
1 you / 15?
  _____   _____
2 you / British?
  _____   _____
3 your mom / a teacher?
  _____   _____
4 your dad / from Canada?
  _____   _____
5 you / happy?
  _____   _____
6 your / classmates / friendly?
  _____   _____

5 ★★☆ **Complete the text messages with the correct form of *to be*.**

Hi Evie. 0____Are____ you happy?
1_____ your new school OK?
2_____ the students friendly?
3_____ it sunny there? It 4_____ sunny here. School 5_____ the same without you. Text me.

Hi Layla. I 6_____ happy. School 7_____ very different here in Australia. There 8_____ ten boys and 12 girls in my class. The girls 9_____ very friendly, but the boys 10_____ . It 11_____ very hot and sunny here. And guess what? There 12_____ a swimming pool in the playground. It 13_____ all bad!

Object pronouns

→ SB p.25

6 ★☆☆ **Complete the sentences with *me*, *him*, *her*, *us*, *you*, and *them*.**

My new school

0 My new school is excellent. I really like _____*it*_____ .

1 The school lunches are great. I like _____ .

2 Our English teacher is Mrs. Davis. I like _____ .

3 We are good students. Mrs. Davis is very happy with _____ .

4 Tim is my best friend here. He's great. I really like _____

5 Are you friendly? Do your classmates like _____ ?

6 I'm friendly. My classmates like _____ .

7 ★★☆ **Complete the dialogues so they are true for you. Use object pronouns.**

0 A Do you like _____*Frenkie de Jong*_____ ? (name of an athlete)

   B Yes, I really like _____*him*_____ .

1 A Do you like _____ ? (name of a female singer)

   B Yes, I like _____ . She's great.

2 A Do you like _____ ? (name of pop group)

   B No, I don't like _____ . They're terrible.

3 A Do you like _____ ? (name of a male actor)

   B Yes, I like _____ . He's an excellent actor.

4 A Do you like _____ ? (name of a comedy movie)

   B Yes, I like _____ . It's very funny.

8 ★★★ **Write questions with *like* and the word in parentheses. Then write answers so they are true for you.**

0 Olivia Rodrigo? (you)
   Do you like Olivia Rodrigo?
   Yes, I like her. She's a great singer.

1 the TV show *Stranger Things*? (you)
   _____
   _____

2 soccer? (your dad)
   _____
   _____

3 Imagine Dragons? (your best friend)
   _____
   _____

4 Cardi B? (you)
   _____
   _____

5 comedy movies? (your mom)
   _____
   _____

6 the song *Dance Monkey* by Tones and I? (you)
   _____
   _____

7 pop music? (your parents)
   _____
   _____

GET IT RIGHT!

Object pronouns

We use *it* in the singular and *them* in the plural.

✓ *I don't want this candy. You take it.*

✓ *I don't want these potato chips. You take them.*

✗ *I don't want these snacks. You take it.*

Circle the correct options.

0 This is my school. I like *it* / *them*.

1 I play computer games. I like *it* / *them*.

2 My dad has a really cool phone. I want *it* / *them*!

3 My country is small, but I like *it* / *them* a lot.

4 Maroon 5? I don't like *it* / *them*.

5 My friends are here. I play soccer with *it* / *them* every afternoon.

6 Here is my homework. I finished *it* / *them* this morning.

ⒶZ VOCABULARY
Adjectives to describe feelings
 SB p.22

1 ★☆☆ **Put the letters in order to make adjectives.**

0 r e d i t   _____tired_____

1 x c e t i e d   _____

2 o r r w i e d   _____

3 y a n g r   _____

4 o r b e d   _____

5 o h t   _____

6 s t y i r t h   _____

7 d a s   _____

8 d l o c   _____

9 g r y n u h   _____

2 ★★☆ **Complete the sentences with the adjectives from Exercise 1.**

0 It's late, and you're _____tired_____ . Go to bed.

1 My new bike is broken. My dad's _____ with me.

2 I'm _____ . Let's play a game on your tablet.

3 My friends are _____ . There's a basketball game at our school today.

4 There's an exam at school today. Amy's _____ .

5 Pedro's dog is sick. He's _____ .

6 I'm hot and _____ . Can I have a drink?

7 He's _____ . He wants a sandwich.

8 It's winter. It's _____ .

9 We're _____ . Let's go for a swim!

3 ★★★ **Circle the correct adjectives.**

0 A Are you (worried) / excited about the exam tomorrow?

   B No, I'm not. It's an easy exam.

1 A Is Ariel excited / bored about the new movie?

   B Yes, she is.

2 A It's cold / hot today. Let's have some ice cream.

   B Yes, OK. That's a good idea.

3 A Are you hungry / thirsty?

   B Yes, I am.

   A Let's have some spaghetti, then.

4 A It's really hot / cold in here.

   B You're right. Let's close the window.

5 A I'm really tired / thirsty.

   B Here's a bottle of water.

   A Thanks.

6 A Mom's angry / sad with you.

   B Why?

   A You're home late.

Positive and negative adjectives   → SB p.25

4 ★★☆ **Put the letters in order to make adjectives.**

0 He's a _____bad_____ actor. (dba)

1 She's a _____ player. (ogod)

2 São Paulo is a _____ city. (arget)

3 The weather today is _____ . (fluwa)

4 It's a _____ TV show. (unfyn)

5 There's an exam today. It's _____ ! (ritlerbe)

6 The sandwiches here are _____ . (etnlcxele)

7 Volleyball is an _____ sport. (igecntix)

5 ★☆☆ **Complete the sentences so they are true for you.**

0 ___Ariana Grande___ is a great singer.

1 _____ is a good book.

2 _____ is a funny actor/actress.

3 _____ is a terrible sport.

4 _____ is a great tennis player.

5 _____ is an exciting city.

6 _____ is an awful computer game.

7 _____ is a bad song.

8 _____ and _____ are excellent games.

6 ★★☆ **Complete the dialogues so they are true for you. Use Yes, I do or No, I don't and an adjective from the list.**

> awful | bad | excellent | exciting
> funny | good | ~~great~~ | terrible

0 A Do you like soccer?

   B ___Yes, I do___ . It's a(n) ___great___ sport.

1 A Do you like swimming?

   B _____ . It's a(n) _____ sport.

2 A Do you like the Harry Potter books?

   B _____ . They're _____ books.

3 A Do you like basketball?

   B _____ . It's a(n) _____ game.

4 A Do you like Patrick Mahomes?

   B _____ . He's a(n) _____ football player.

5 A Do you like the Spider-Man movies?

   B _____ . They're _____ movies.

PRONUNCIATION
Vowel sounds – adjectives   Go to page 118. 🎧

REFERENCE

ADJECTIVES TO DESCRIBE FEELINGS

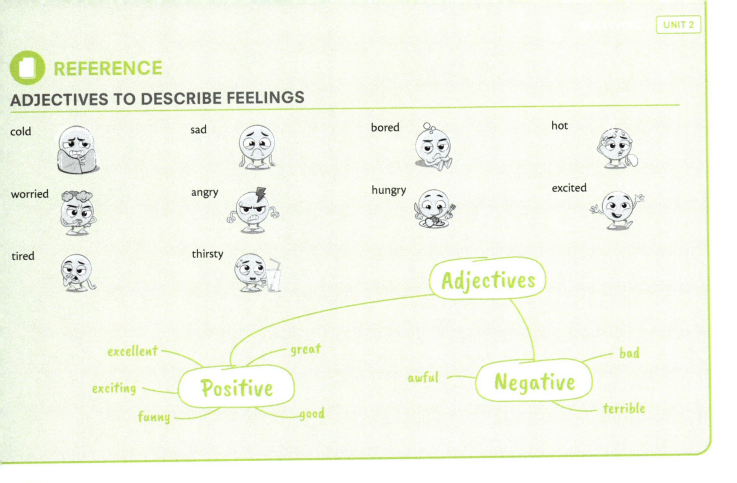

cold

sad

bored

hot

worried

angry

hungry

excited

tired

thirsty

Adjectives

Positive — excellent, great, exciting, funny, good

Negative — awful, bad, terrible

VOCABULARY *EXTRA*

1 Match the pictures with an adjective from the list.

> afraid | difficult | easy | happy | heavy | strong

0 ___afraid___

1 _____

2 _____

3 _____

4 _____

5 _____

2 Complete the sentences with the correct adjective from Exercise 1.

1 A lot of people find math _____ .

2 Mei is _____ today – it's her birthday.

3 Some children are _____ of the dark at night.

4 My mom's suitcase is _____ – it's 23 kg!

5 Rugby players are very _____ .

6 It's _____ to make a cup of tea.

A young star

NAME: Grace Avery VanderWaal

NATIONALITY: American

PLACE OF BIRTH: Lenaxa, Kansas, US

LIKES: movies, music, books

The year is 2020. Grace VanderWaal is at school in Suffern, New York. She's 15, and she's excited. She loves high school and her friends there. Grace is a winner of the TV show *America's Got Talent*. Her parents are not musicians. Her mother's name is Tina, and her father's name is David. Grace has a brother named Jakob and a sister named Olivia. Grace is a pop singer. She plays the ukulele and writes her own songs. She's also an actress in a Disney movie named *Stargirl*. Her YouTube channel is famous, and she plays with groups like Imagine Dragons and Florence and the Machine. Her music is popular in the US, Europe, Australia, and Japan. Maybe it's popular in your country, too!

WHO ARE HER MUSICAL HEROES?

Jason Mraz and Katy Perry

DOES SHE LIKE SOCIAL MEDIA?

Yes, she does. She's on Facebook and Instagram and has millions of followers.

WHAT DOES SHE LIKE?

Grace likes movies (her favorite is *Breakfast at Tiffany's*), reading, writing songs, and school!

READING

1 **Read the profile of a young singer. Find and <u>underline</u> the answers to these questions.**

  1 Why is she famous?

  2 Which movie is she in?

2 **Read the profile again and write short answers to the questions.**

  0 Is her nationality British?   *No, it isn't.*

  1 Is Grace happy at school?   _____

  2 Is Grace from New York?   _____

  3 Are her parents musicians?   _____

  4 Is she an actress?   _____

  5 Does she like Jason Mraz?   _____

  6 Does she like movies?   _____

  7 Are songs important to her?   _____

  8 Is she popular in your country?   _____

3 **CRITICAL THINKING** **Read the text again. Mark the sentences T (true) or F (false) for Grace.**

  1 I think high school is great. ☐

  2 All my family are good musicians. ☐

  3 I am only good at singing. ☐

  4 The old movies are the best! ☐

DEVELOPING Writing

A text message

1 **INPUT** Read the text messages and write P (positive) or N (negative) below each message.

a Hi, Diana. Are you still bored? Read a book! My favorite book is *Little Women*. It's a great story. I really like Jo. She's friendly and funny. Sometimes it's sad 😞 , but the ending is happy 😃 ! Please read it.

Naomi ☐

b Hi, Mark. I'm at the movies. The movie is terrible. I don't like it. The actors are very bad. I don't like them. I'm really bored. Where are you? Text me.

Toni ☐

c Hi, Josh. Are you at home? Listen to this song. It's great! The singer is excellent. The guitarist is good. I really like it. Do you? Tell me what you think.

Lara ☐

d Hi, Sam. Thank you for the movie. It's very funny. I really like it. My sister likes it, too. Rebel Wilson is great! She's a very funny actress. The other actors are good, too. Talk soon.

Daisy ☐

e Hi, Patri. This song is terrible! How is it number one? The singer is awful, and the words are boring. I really don't like it. My friends don't like it. Why is it popular? What do you think? Text me!!!

Adam ☐

2 **ANALYZE** Find and write all of the adjectives from Exercise 1 in the correct columns.

positive	negative

3 Look at the text messages in Exercise 1. Complete the sentences with *likes* or *doesn't like* and the correct adjective.

0 Naomi ___likes___ the story. It's ___great___ .
1 Toni _____ the movie. It's _____ .
2 Lara _____ the song. It's _____ .
3 Daisy _____ the movie. It's _____ .
4 Adam _____ the song. It's _____ .

4 You like a book, and you want to text a friend about it. Complete the text message.

Hi, _____ . Are you still bored?
Read a book! My favorite book is
_____ . It's a _____ story. I really
like _____ . He/She is _____ .
The ending is _____ . Please read it.

5 You don't like a movie, and you want to text a friend about it. Complete the text message.

Hi, _____ . I'm at the movies. The movie
is _____ . I _____ it. The actors are
_____ . I _____ them. I'm really
_____ . Where are you? Text me.

6 **PLAN** Think about a movie, a book, a band, or a song and write notes about it.

Title: _____
like / don't like   great / terrible
_____
_____
_____

✏️ WRITING TIP: Some useful language

- I *like* / *don't like* the movie.
- I *really like* / *love* the song.
- The *movie* / *book* / *band* / *song* is *funny* / *exciting* / *sad*.
- The *actor(s)* / *singer(s)* is / are *great* / *terrible* / *awful*.
- The ending is *happy* / *sad*.

7 **PRODUCE** Now write a short text message about the movie, book, band, or song. Use your notes from Exercise 6. Write 35–50 words.

_____
_____
_____
_____

1 🔊 2.03 **Listen to the conversations.**
Which conversation (1–5) matches the photo?
Write the number.

2 🔊 2.03 **Listen again and mark the sentences**
T (true) or F (false).

1 It's Emma's birthday. ☐
2 Tom is cold. ☐
3 John doesn't like English. ☐
4 Tyler doesn't like the movie. ☐
5 Helen's cat is sick. ☐

3 🔊 2.03 **Listen again and circle the correct**
options.

1 **A** Hi, Jane.
  B Oh, hi, Kate.
  A It's Emma's birthday today. Is she *happy* / *excited*?
  B Yes, she is. I'm *happy* / *excited*, too.
2 **A** What's the matter?
  B It's *hot* / *cold* in here. Are you *hot* / *cold*, Tom?
  A *No, I'm not.* / *Yes, I am.* I'm wearing a sweater.
  B Well, I'm very *hot* / *cold*. Can you *open* / *close* the window?
  A OK.
3 **A** There's an exam tomorrow. Are you worried, John?
  B No, I'm not worried about it. I *like* / *don't like* English. I'm just tired.
  A Well, I'm worried. I'm very worried. I *like* / *don't like* English.
4 **A** What's wrong, Tyler? Are you *tired* / *bored*?
  B No, I'm not. I'm just *tired* / *bored*. I don't like this movie.
  A Why? I *like* / *don't like* it. It's very funny.
5 **A** What's the matter with Helen? Why is she *sad* / *angry*?
  B Her cat's sick. It's at the vet.
  A Oh, no. That's *sad* / *terrible*. Poor Helen.

DIALOGUE

4 **Complete the conversation with the words from**
the list.

> don't like | funny | great | ~~likes~~ | likes | terrible

A Do you like the song *Can You Feel the Love Tonight?* from the movie *The Lion King*?
B No, I don't. But my little sister ⁰___*likes*___ it. It's her favorite song. She sings it all the time. In fact, she ¹_____ all the songs from the movie.
A Do you like the movie?
B No, I don't. It's ²_____ . I ³_____ kids' movies.
A Ah, I really like it. It's a ⁴_____ movie. It's ⁵_____ .

Train to TH!NK

Categorizing

5 **Put the words in the list into categories.**
There are four words for each category.

> beach | ~~Brazil~~ | cold | museum
> New Zealand | sad | school | stadium
> the US | thirsty | tired | Turkey

Countries	Feelings	Places
Brazil		

6 **Choose words that you know and put them into**
these three categories.

Nationalities	Colors	Classroom things

7 **Name these three categories.**

1 _____	2 _____	3 _____
good	fourteen	Laura
great	sixty-three	Tim
terrible	one hundred	Katy

EXAM SKILLS: READING
Skimming

📖 READING TIP

- Read the questions first. Then read the text quickly.
- Think about what type of text it is. Is it an article from a newspaper? An email? A text message?
- Underline the 'important' words, such as adjectives, nouns and verbs.
- Try to answer *Wh-* questions – *Who, What, When* and *Where*.

1 Skim the text in Exercise 4. What type of text is it?

A a newspaper article ☐
B an email ☐
C a text message ☐

2 Find and write these 'important' words from the text.

two adjectives to describe feelings

_____

_____

two positive adjectives

_____

_____

two negative adjectives

_____

_____

3 Complete the table with information about the text.

Who?	1 _____
What?	2 _____
When?	3 _____
Where?	4 _____

4 Read the text again and choose the correct answers (A or B).

🎧 **Lucy**
Samara@thinkmail.com

Hi Lucy,

I'm bored. It's my little brother Jaden's birthday today. He's eight. He's very excited. All his friends are here. It's hot and sunny. They're in the garden now. His friends from his school football team are here. So, of course, they all like football. His favourite team is Liverpool. I like Liverpool, too. They're an excellent team.

Guess what his present from me is? It's a FIFA World Cup football! Oh, and a book – *Kai and the Monkey King*. It's a great story and I really like the pictures. They're excellent.

His presents from Mum and Dad are a bike and a film. It's a really good bike, but the film is terrible. It's called *Ant-Man 2*. I don't like the Ant-man films. They aren't funny.

It's 11 o'clock – Jaden's birthday lunch is in two hours. There's a big birthday cake, too. But I'm hungry now!

See you soon,

Samara

0 Is Samara excited?
A Yes, she is.
Ⓑ No, she isn't.

1 Is it her brother's birthday today?
A Yes, it is.
B No, it isn't.

2 Is it a hot day?
A Yes, it is.
B No, it isn't.

3 Samara _____ Liverpool.
A likes
B doesn't like

4 *Kai and the Monkey King* is a/an _____ book.
A awful
B great

5 Samara doesn't like the *Ant-Man* films.
They _____ funny.
A are
B aren't

6 Is Samara thirsty?
A Yes, she is.
B No, she isn't.

CONSOLIDATION

🎧 LISTENING

1 🔊 2.04 **Listen to Annie. Circle the correct answers (A, B, or C).**

1 Annie is from ...
   A the US.
   B South Africa.
   C Mexico.
2 She's ...
   A 12.
   B 13.
   C 14.
3 Her best friend is from ...
   A Brazil.
   B South Africa.
   C the UK.
4 Her best friend is named ...
   A Paulo.
   B Pedro.
   C Marcel.

2 🔊 2.04 **Listen again. Mark the sentences T (true) or F (false).**

1 Annie is from Cape Town. ☐
2 She doesn't like sports. ☐
3 Her favorite athlete is a tennis player. ☐
4 Her favorite singer is Taylor Swift. ☐
5 Her best friend is Spanish. ☐
6 Her best friend is the same age as her. ☐

🔤 VOCABULARY

3 **Complete the sentences with words from the list. There are two extra words.**

> angry | exciting | expensive | fast | hungry | Japan
> Japanese | old | Russian | terrible | thirsty | tired

1 Singing lessons aren't cheap. They're _____ .
2 Akemi is from Japan. She's _____ .
3 Maxim is from Moscow. He's _____ .
4 The car isn't _____ . It's very slow.
5 My phone is _____ . It isn't new.
6 Dad is _____ . He isn't happy.
7 It's very late. I'm really _____ . Good night.
8 Water? Yes, please. I'm really _____ .
9 The new Avengers movie is really good. It's so _____ !
10 That new restaurant is bad. The food is _____ .

Ⓖ GRAMMAR

4 **Complete the dialogues with the missing words.**

1 A Do ⁰___you___ like chocolate cake?
   B Yes, I love ¹_____ .
2 A ²_____ you like snakes?
   B No, I don't like ³_____ .
3 A Do you like Vanessa?
   B Yes, I like ⁴_____ . ⁵_____ is my best friend.
4 A Do you like Mr. Henderson?
   B No, I don't like ⁶_____ . ⁷_____ 's boring.

5 **Complete the sentences with the correct form of to be. Use contracted forms where possible.**

0 I'm not Spanish. I ____'m____ Argentinian.
1 I _____ (✗) ten years old. I _____ 11.
2 A _____ Danny happy?
   B No, he _____ .
3 Jason and Kylie _____ from Australia.
4 A _____ you hungry?
   B Yes, we _____ .
5 Martina _____ (✗) 12. She _____ 11.
6 A Why _____ you angry?
   B Because you _____ late.
7 A How old _____ they?
   B Kevin _____ five, and Gemma _____ eight.
8 A Where _____ Cathy from?
   B She _____ from South Africa.

DIALOGUE

6  **Put the conversation in order.
Then listen and check.**

- ☐ **Izzy** I'm great. It's my birthday today.
- ☐ **Izzy** I know. I'm really excited.
- ☐ **Izzy** Bye.
- ☐ **Izzy** Thanks. I'm off to the new Italian restaurant.
- ☐ **Izzy** Hi, Sam, how's it going?
- ☐ **Sam** Well, have fun. See you later.
- ☐ **Sam** That is so awesome! Happy birthday!
- ☐ **Sam** Oh, hi, Izzy. I'm fine. How about you?
- ☐ **Sam** The new Italian restaurant? It's great.

📖 READING

7 **Read the text about Rishi. Complete the
information in the form.**

Personal information

Name: ⁰ _Rishi Singh_
Age: ¹_____
Nationality: ²_____
Likes: ³_____
Favorite athlete: ⁴_____
Favorite singer: ⁵_____
Best friend: ⁶_____

My name is Rishi Singh. I'm 13 years old.
I'm from the US. I live in Boston.
I really like sports. I like swimming
and soccer. My favorite athlete is Kevin
de Bruyne. He's a soccer player from
Belgium. He's a midfielder, and he's great.
I also like music. My favorite singer is
Stormzy. He's a British singer. He's really
good. My best friend is Nicole. She's 13,
and she's at my school.

8 **Read the text again and correct the sentences.**

0 Rishi is from the UK.
   Rishi is from the US.

1 Rishi's hometown is New York.
   _____

2 Rishi really likes basketball.
   _____

3 Kevin de Bruyne is a tennis player.
   _____

4 Rishi's favorite singer is a woman.
   _____

5 Rishi's best friend is a boy.
   _____

6 Nicole is 12.
   _____

7 Nicole isn't at his school.
   _____

✏️ WRITING

9 **Write a short text about you. Write 35–50 words.
Use the questions to help you.**

- What is your name?
- How old are you?
- Where you are from and what is your nationality?
- What do you like?
- Who is your favorite athlete?
- Who is your favorite singer?
- Who is your best friend?

_____
_____
_____
_____
_____

3 FAMILY TIME

→ 08

Grammar rap!

GRAMMAR
Possessive 's

→ SB p.32

1 ★☆☆ **Follow the lines and complete the sentences. Use 's.**

grandfather

Jason

Eva

grandmother

mother

Grayson

Anya

0 It's my _____*grandfather's*_____ bike.

1 It's _____ scooter.

2 It's _____ tennis racket.

3 It's my _____ book.

4 It's my _____ car.

5 It's _____ tablet.

6 It's _____ phone.

Possessive adjectives

→ SB p.33

2 ★☆☆ **Complete the table.**

	Possessive adjective	
I	0	*my*
you	1	
he	2	
she	3	
we	4	
they	5	

3 ★★☆ **Joe and Nicky are at a birthday party. Circle the correct possessive adjective.**

Joe Hi! What's ¹*your* / *his* name?

Nicky Nicky.

Joe Is that girl ²*her* / *your* friend?

Nicky Well, no. That's ³*my* / *their* sister. ⁴*His* / *Her* name's Macy. This is ⁵*our* / *your* house.

Joe Oh. And who are those two boys?

Nicky They're ⁶*your* / *my* brothers. They're twins. They're 12 today. It's ⁷*their* / *our* birthday party. Wait a minute. Who are you?

Joe I'm Joe. I'm here with Marco. I'm ⁸*her* / *his* cousin.

Nicky Oh, right.

4 ★★☆ **Complete the sentences with the correct possessive pronoun.**

0 It's George's rabbit. It's _____*his*_____ rabbit.

1 It's my mother's book. It's _____ book.

2 They're Jenny's cookies. They're _____ cookies.

3 It's Patty and Sonia's tablet. It's _____ tablet.

4 It's my and my brother's TV. It's _____ TV.

5 They're Jamie's headphones. They're _____ headphones.

6 It's my grandfather's chair. It's _____ chair.

7 I have three cousins – that's _____ house.

8 That's my family's car. It's _____ car.

9 **A** Is that _____ phone on the table?

  B No, this is _____ phone in my hand.

10 **A** Is _____ friend's name Nina?

  B No, _____ name is Lena.

this / that / these / those

 → SB p.34

5 ★★☆ (Circle) **the correct answers (A, B, or C).**

0 _____ is my bedroom.

  (A) This **B** These **C** Those

1 _____ is my new gaming console.

  A Those **B** That **C** These

2 _____ are photos of my cat.

  A That **B** These **C** This

3 _____ computer on the table is my sister's.

  A Those **B** These **C** That

4 Are _____ your books over there?

  A these **B** that **C** those

5 Is _____ a good movie?

  A these **B** this **C** those

6 _____ boys are from Colombia.

  A This **B** That **C** Those

7 _____ hotel is very expensive.

  A That **B** Those **C** These

8 _____ computer here is really slow.

  A That **B** This **C** These

9 Are _____ soccer players Spanish?

  A this **B** these **C** that

10 Is _____ his pen?

  A these **B** those **C** this

6 ★★☆ **Complete the sentences with *this*, *that*, *these*, or *those*.**

0 _____*These*_____ are the books I want, here.

1 _____ are my friends, over there.

2 _____ is my new phone, just here.

3 _____ are my new video games, here.

4 _____ is my father, over there.

5 _____ is my bed, right here.

6 _____ are my cousins, there.

7 _____ is my brother's laptop, right here.

8 _____ are my headphones, here.

GET IT RIGHT!

this and these

We use *this* to talk about singular objects that are near to us. We use *these* to talk about plural objects that are near to us.

✓ *This is my favorite dress.*

✗ ~~These~~ *is my favorite dress.*

✓ *These are my shoes.*

✗ ~~This~~ *are my shoes.*

Complete the sentences with *this* or *these*.

0 He gave me _____*this*_____ shirt.

1 Is _____ your pencil?

2 _____ are my favorite snacks.

3 I got _____ book yesterday.

4 Are _____ your computer games?

5 _____ are my old sneakers.

6 I like _____ photo.

PRONUNCIATION

this / that / these / those Go to page 118.

🄐 VOCABULARY
Family members

→ SB p.32

1 ★☆☆ **Complete the words.**

0 au_n_t
1 _ _ o _ _
2 _ _ o _ _ e _
3 _ u _ _ a _ _ _
4 _ i _ e
5 _ ou _ i _
6 _ _ a _ _ _ _ o _ _ e _
7 _ _ a _ _ _ a _ _ e _
8 _ _ a _ _ _ _ o _

2 ★★☆ **Complete the sentences and the crossword with the same word. What's the mystery word?**

```
1 [ ][O][ ][ ][ ][ ]
2    [ ][T][ ][ ]
3    [ ][S][ ][ ][ ]
4    [ ][ ][ ][H][ ][ ]
5 [ ][ ][ ][E][ ]
6 [ ][ ][ ][E][ ]
7    [ ][ ][G][ ][ ][ ]
```

1 My _____ is 45. She's a teacher.
2 My _____ Sophia is my mother's sister.
3 My little _____ is only five years old.
4 I'm 12, and my_____ is 14.
5 My _____ is from London. He's English.
6 My _____ José is from Brazil.
7 Our teacher's _____ is a student in our class.

3 ★★★ **Write answers to the questions so they are true for you.**

1 Is your family big or small?

_____

2 What are your parents' names?

_____

3 How many cousins do you have?

_____

4 How many aunts and uncles do you have?

_____

5 Where do the people in your family live?

_____

6 How many people do you live with?

_____

House and furniture

→ SB p.35

4 ★☆☆ **Circle the odd one out in each list.**

0 bath   shower   (sofa)
1 armchair   bedroom   kitchen
2 shower   hall   dining room
3 stove   bed   fridge
4 bedroom   toilet   living room
5 garage   kitchen   yard
6 car   hall   kitchen

5 ★★☆ **Look at the photos. Where in a house are these things? Write the words.**

0 _living room_

1 _____

2 _____

3 _____

4 _____

5 _____

6 ★★★ **Are these things in the correct place? Mark them ✓ (yes, OK) or ✗ (no).**

1 a shower in the kitchen ☐
2 a sofa in the bedroom ☐
3 a car in the garage ☐
4 a fridge in the bedroom ☐
5 an oven in the garage ☐
6 a car in the hall ☐
7 a toilet in the bathroom ☐
8 an armchair in the yard ☐

REFERENCE
Family members

MALE	FEMALE
son	daughter
father	mother
brother	sister
grandfather	grandmother
uncle	aunt
husband	wife
grandson	granddaughter
cousin	cousin

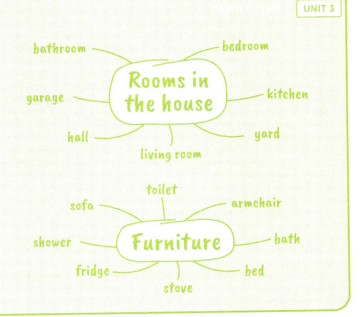

VOCABULARY *EXTRA*

1 **Label the drawing with the words from the list.**

cup | fork | glass | knife | plate | spoon

0 ___cup___

1 _____

2 _____

3 _____

4 _____

5 _____

2 **Find the words from Exercise 1 in the word snake.**

complatesuppespoonanorglasshapcupetbknifequesforkpose

PHOTO 1 _____

It's my 13th birthday today. Look! Here's my cake. I'm here at my favorite restaurant in Buenos Aires with my brothers Thiago and Nico. Thiago's my twin, so it's his birthday, too. Nico's the baby of the family. He's five.

PHOTO 2 _____

This is my grandfather's 75th birthday party. My mom and dad, three aunts, one uncle, and six cousins are all here. Aunt Claudia is my favorite aunt. She's my mother's sister. She lives in Canada with her husband Sheldon. He's Canadian. They are teachers at Toronto University. My dad's a teacher, too, and my mom's a doctor.

PHOTO 3 _____

Our house isn't big, but I have my own bedroom. It's small, but I love it! Do you like it? I have a desk for my laptop and a chair, and there's a bed, of course! I also have a closet for my clothes. Thiago and Nico's bedroom is big, with two beds and Thiago's guitar.

PHOTO 4 _____

Here's Luna, my beautiful rabbit, with Thiago's cat. Luna's a friendly rabbit, but she's very big. The cat's name is Chester. He's very small. Luna and Chester are very good friends.

📖 READING

1 **Read the social media posts quickly. Is Emilia's family big or small?**

2 **Read the posts again and complete the sentences with words from the text.**

0 Emilia has two ___*brothers*___ , Thiago and Nico.
1 It's Emilia and Thiago's 13th birthday. They are _____ .
2 Claudia is Emilia's favorite _____ .
3 Sheldon is from _____ .
4 Emilia's mother is a _____ .
5 Emilia's bedroom is _____ .
6 Emilia has a _____ for her clothes.
7 Her brothers have two _____ in their room.
8 Luna the rabbit is big, but she's _____ .

3 **CRITICAL THINKING** **Choose a title for each photo from the list and write it under the photo.**

So sweet | Love my family! | Home sweet home
I'm a teenager!

DEVELOPING ⟩ *Writing*

My bedroom

1 **INPUT** **Read the text. Find five differences between Jake's perfect bedroom and his real bedroom.**

MY **PERFECT BEDROOM** AND MY **REAL BEDROOM**

My perfect bedroom is big. The walls are green, and the floor is brown. The bed is very big – it's 2 meters long and 1.6 meters wide (I like big beds!). It's very comfortable, too, and it's the color that my favorite soccer team plays in. So, it's black and white because my favorite team is Juventus. The desk is near the window and has a comfortable chair for me to sit in when I work on my fantastic new computer.

My real bedroom isn't big. The floor is brown, but the walls are blue. The bed is OK, but it isn't very big, and it isn't very comfortable! The bed is black and white – yay! My desk is near the door, and the chair is small, but it's OK. And I like my computer. It's old, but it's really good!

2 **ANALYZE** **Complete the sentences with *and* or *but*.**

0 The walls are red, _____*and*_____ the floor is black.

1 The bed isn't very big, _____ it's comfortable.

2 The bed is comfortable, _____ it's in Real Madrid colors, too.

3 The computer is old, _____ it's really good.

3 **PLAN** **Think about your real bedroom and about your perfect bedroom. Make notes about them.**

	My real bedroom	My perfect bedroom
big / small?		
wall color?		
floor color?		
big / small bed? comfortable?		
bed color?		
near the window?		
chair? desk?		

 **WRITING TIP: Spelling**

When writing your description, always check that you have the correct spelling, especially for new words.

4 **PRODUCE** **Use your notes to write about your real bedroom. Then use your completed text and your notes to write sentences about your perfect bedroom. Write 35–50 words.**

My real bedroom

My real bedroom _____ big.
The floor is _____ , and the walls are
_____ . The bed is _____ .
The bed is _____ .
The _____ is near the window.
The _____ is _____ .

My perfect bedroom

_____
_____
_____
_____
_____
_____
_____

LISTENING

1 🔊 **3.03** **Listen to the conversation and complete the sentences. Write *Tony*, *Christine*, or *Jack*.**

0 _____*Christine*_____ says the room is nice.
1 _____ is Tony's brother.
2 _____ likes watching soccer.
3 _____ loves movies.
4 The games are _____'s.

2 🔊 **3.03** **Listen again and complete the words in this part of the conversation.**

Christine Wow! Are these your DVDs, Tony?
They're ⁰g___*reat*___! I ¹l_____
movies.

Tony No, they're my brother's. He really
²l_____ old movies. Very, very old
movies.

Christine ³W_____ a ⁴n_____ collection!

Tony Yeah. It's not bad. But the movies are a
little boring!

Christine No, they're great! Hey! Are these your games?
They're ⁵f_____! This one
⁶i_____ really ⁷c_____!

Tony Yeah, I ⁸r_____ ⁹l_____ Fortnite.
It's my favorite. It's a great game.

Christine Let's play it now!

Tony OK.

DIALOGUE

3 **Put the conversations in order.**

Conversation 1

☐ **Julia** Yes, it is cool. I love T-shirts!

☐ **Julia** Happy birthday, Sienna! This is a present
for you.

☐ **Julia** This one? It's from Spain. It's a birthday
present from my Spanish friend.

☐ **Sienna** For me? Thanks, Julia! Oh, a T-shirt! And it's
really cool!

☐ **Sienna** Your T-shirt's nice, too. I really like it.

Conversation 2

☐ **Ali** Is your brother there, too?

☐ **Ali** Hi, Juan. Thanks. Wow, I really like
your house.

☐ **Juan** Thank you! Come into the living room.
My mom and dad are there.

☐ **Juan** Hi, Ali! Nice to see you. Come in!

☐ **Juan** No, he isn't. He's in his bedroom.

4 **Look at Exercise 3 and complete the conversations between you and a friend.**

Conversation 1

You I really ¹*like* / *love* your T-shirt. Is it new?

Friend Yes, it's from ²_____ .

You It looks ³*great* / *nice* / *fantastic*.

Friend Thanks.

Conversation 2

You What ⁴*cool* / *great* / *fantastic* music!

Friend Yes, it's ⁵_____ .

You I really ⁶*like* / *love* it.

Friend Let's listen to more music now.

Conversation 3

You What a ⁷*fantastic* / *good* / *great* computer game!

Friend Yes. It's called ⁸_____ .

You I really ⁹*love* / *like* computer games.

Friend OK. Let's play it together!

5 **Now write your own conversation.**

PHRASES FOR FLUENCY → SB p.36

6 **Complete the phrases with the missing vowels.**

0 R_e_ _a_lly?
1 __h, r__ght.
2 L__t's g__ .
3 J__st __ m__n__t__ .

7 **Complete the conversation with the phrases from Exercise 6.**

Aida That boy over there is really nice.

Jon ⁰_____*Really*_____ ? Him? Well, he isn't
my favorite person.

Aida I think he looks really cool.

Jon Well, he is, but sometimes he's difficult.

Aida Hey, ¹_____ . Isn't he in your family?

Jon Yes, he's my brother.

Aida ²_____ .
Your brother. OK.

Jon Aida, ³_____ !
We're late for class!

SUM IT UP

1 Look at the pictures and complete the crossword.

S	T	O	V	E

ACROSS   DOWN

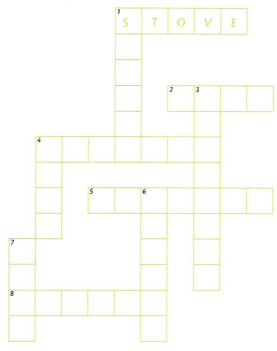

2 Read a webpage about a famous house. Who lives there?

Chatsworth House

Visit Chatsworth House! This famous house is over 450 years old. The Duke of Devonshire (he's the 12th Duke) lives here with his wife and three children, but Chatsworth House is also open for visitors. The house has over 200 rooms, 17 modern bathrooms, and 459 windows. Walk around the house and imagine you are a king or a queen. See the beautiful painted hall, the state dining room, the library, and bedrooms. Walk in the lovely gardens. See the farm with cows, sheep, and horses!

i Open from March to May and September to November, 11:00–5:00 every day. Tickets are £24.00 per adult and £14.50 for children, or £66.00 for a family of four or more.

3 Complete the notes with information from the webpage.

Age of house	0	*450 years old*
Family name	1	
Number of rooms	2	
Number of windows	3	
Animals on farm	4	
Opening time	5	
Closing time	6	
Months open	7	
Price per child	8	
Price for a family (4+)	9	

Grammar rap!

@ GRAMMAR
there is / there are
→ SB p.40

1 ★☆☆ **Complete the sentences with *is* or *are*.**

0 There _____*are*_____ four bedrooms in the house.

1 There _____ two Colombian girls at our school.

2 There _____ lots of famous squares in Paris.

3 There _____ a mountain near Tokyo called Mount Fuji.

4 _____ there a desk in your bedroom?

5 There _____ a small TV in my parents' bedroom.

6 There _____ nine or ten big train stations in London.

7 There _____ eight people in my family.

8 _____ there any good stores here?

2 ★★☆ **Complete the text with *there is*, *there isn't*, *there are*, or *there aren't*.**

> Julia is 14. Here is what she says about Roseland, her local shopping center.

"I really like our local shopping center. It's small, but ⁰_____*there is*_____ a movie theater. ¹_____ some cafés on the top floor, but ²_____ any restaurants. My mom likes it because ³_____ two good bookstores, and ⁴_____ a great supermarket. My brother likes it because ⁵_____ some cool clothes stores. My dad doesn't like it because ⁶_____ a good sporting goods store (and he loves sports!). My sister doesn't like shopping."

some / any
→ SB p.40

3 ★☆☆ **Circle the correct options.**

0 There are (some) / any books in my room.

1 There aren't some / any good stores here.

2 There are some / any nice curtains in their house.

3 There aren't some / any interesting books in the library.

4 There aren't some / any banks on this street.

5 There are some / any fantastic things in the museum.

6 There aren't some / any cafés in the park.

7 There are some / any supermarkets in this neighborhood.

8 There are some / any chairs in the yard.

4 ★★☆ **Complete the sentences with *some* or *any*.**

0 There are _____*some*_____ good stores.

1 There aren't _____ sporting goods stores.

2 There aren't _____ movie theaters.

3 There are _____ clothes stores.

4 There aren't _____ phone stores.

5 There are _____ cafés.

5 ★★☆ **Complete the text with *there is a*, *there isn't a*, *there are some*, or *there aren't any*.**

> Kevin is 12. This is what he thinks of Parkwood, his local shopping center.

"The shopping center near my house is really big. There are about 200 stores in it. ⁰____*There is a*____ fantastic food court. ¹_____ café with great ice cream. I like it because ²_____ good movie theater and a library, too. Mom says ³_____ good shoe stores, but they're not my favorite places. ⁴_____ video game stores, and ⁵_____ great clothes stores. The only bad things are that ⁶_____ electronics stores, and ⁷_____ good restaurants."

6 ★★★ **Complete the questions with *Is there a / an* or *Are there any*. Then look at the texts in Exercises 2 and 5 and answer the questions. Use *Yes, there is / are*, *No, there isn't / aren't*, or *I don't know*.**

0 _____*Is there a*_____ supermarket in Roseland?
_____*Yes, there is.*_____

1 _____ movie theaters in Roseland?
_____

2 _____ electronics stores in Roseland?
_____

3 _____ clothes stores in Roseland?
_____

4 _____ sporting goods stores in Roseland?
_____

5 _____ bank in Parkwood?
_____

6 _____ café in Parkwood?
_____

7 _____ library in Parkwood?
_____

8 _____ music stores in Parkwood?
_____

9 _____ good restaurants in Parkwood?
_____

7 ★★★ **Complete these sentences so they are true for a shopping center that you go to.**

1 There are _____ .
2 There aren't _____ .
3 There aren't _____ .
4 There are _____ .
5 There is _____ .
6 There isn't _____ .

Imperatives

→ SB p.41

8 ★☆☆ Ⓒircle **the correct options.**

0 OK, everyone. Please (listen) / *don't listen* to me.
This is important.

1 Are you tired? *Go / Don't go* to bed late tonight.

2 Please *be / don't be* quiet in the library.

3 It's cold in here. *Open / Don't open* the window, please.

4 Hello. Please come in and *sit / don't sit* down.

5 Wow! *Look / Don't look* at that fantastic statue.

6 It's a very expensive store! *Buy / Don't buy* your new clothes there!

7 To get to the movie theater, *turn / don't turn* left at the supermarket, and it's there.

8 *Listen / Don't listen* to your brother.
He's wrong.

9 ★★☆ **Mack and Josh are looking for a sporting goods store. Complete the dialogue with the words from the list.**

go | listen to | look | open | sit down | turn

Mack Where's the sporting goods store?

Josh OK, 0 _____*sit down*_____ on this chair and
¹ _____ at the map.

Mack I don't have a map.

Josh Oh, well I have an app.

Mack Well ² _____ the app on your phone, then.

Josh OK, OK. Wait a minute. Oh! Look, there's the sporting goods store. ³ _____ down here and ⁴ _____ left. The sporting goods store is behind the pharmacy.

Mack Is it across from the phone store?

Josh No, ⁵ _____ me, Mack!
It's on the corner, behind the pharmacy.

GET IT RIGHT!

some and *any*

We use *some* in affirmative sentences and *any* in negative sentences.

✓ *I have some time.*
✗ *I have any time.*
✓ *He doesn't have any money.*
✗ *He doesn't have some money.*

Complete the sentences with *some* or *any*.

0 I don't have _____*any*_____ pets.
1 There are _____ good games.
2 Don't bring _____ food.
3 They don't have _____ homework.
4 I have _____ time.
5 I have _____ presents for you.
6 We don't have _____ problems.

VOCABULARY
Places in a town/city
→ SB p.40

1 ★★☆ **Where are these people? Write a word from the list.**

bank | library | museum | park | pharmacy
~~post office~~ | restaurant | supermarket | train station

0 Hi I need to send this letter to Australia, please.
___*post office*___

1 We need some apples and bananas.
_____

2 Look! These paintings are 200 years old!
_____

3 A round-trip ticket to Chicago, please.
_____

4 Please be quiet in here. People are reading.
_____

5 It's a great day for a picnic here.
_____

6 Hi. Can I exchange these dollars for pounds, please?
_____

7 The steak salad for me, please.
_____

8 I need some medicine for my eye.
_____

Prepositions of place
→ SB p.41

2 ★☆☆ **Look at the map of the shopping center and circle the correct option.**

movie theater

0 The electronics store is *behind* / *next to* the bank.
1 The electronics store is *between* / *in front of* the bank and the bookstore.
2 The bookstore is *across from* / *on the corner*.
3 The shoe store is *between* / *across from* the supermarket.
4 The bank is *next to* / *behind* the shoe store.
5 The café is *behind* / *in front of* the movie theater.

PRONUNCIATION
Word stress in numbers Go to page 119.

38

3 ★★☆ **Look at the map again. Use the prepositions in Exercise 2 to complete the sentences.**

0 The pharmacy is ___*next to*___ the supermarket.
1 The restaurant is _____ the shoe store.
2 The post office is _____ the restaurant and the phone store.
3 The restaurant is _____ the supermarket.
4 The sporting goods store is _____ the pharmacy.
5 The movie theater is _____ the café.
6 The phone store is _____ the bookstore.

Numbers 100+
→ SB p.42

4 ★☆☆ **Write the words or numbers.**

0 ___110___ ___*one hundred ten*___
1 _____ one hundred seventeen
2 125 _____
3 _____ one hundred ninety-eight
4 215 _____
5 _____ three hundred twelve
6 652 _____
7 _____ one thousand three hundred
8 1,400 _____
9 _____ two thousand six hundred twenty

Prices
→ SB p.43

0 ___*twelve fifty*___   **3** _____

1 _____   **4** _____

2 _____   **5** _____

5 ★★☆ **Write the prices in words.**

6 ★★★ **Write the name of places/things you know.**

1 a famous tower   _____
2 a good shoe store   _____
3 a famous square   _____
4 a statue of a famous person _____
5 a famous palace   _____

REFERENCE

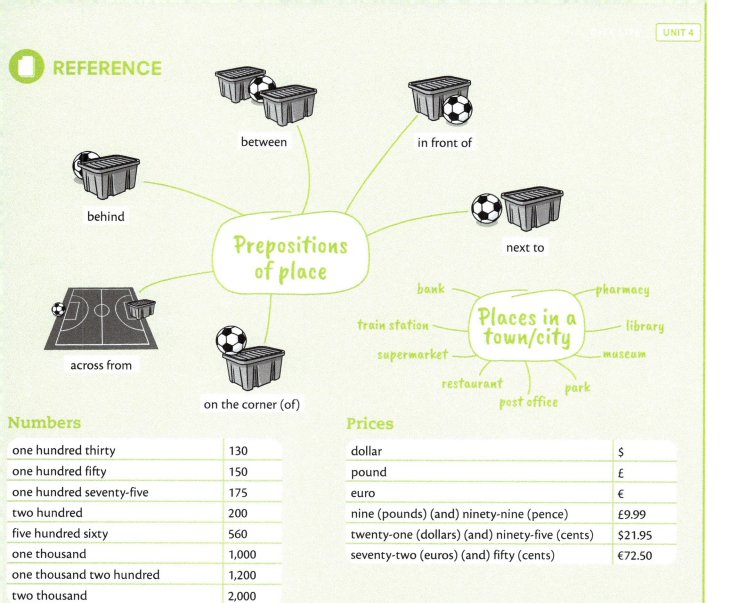

Prepositions of place

between

in front of

behind

next to

across from

on the corner (of)

Places in a town/city

bank · pharmacy · train station · library · supermarket · museum · restaurant · park · post office

Numbers

one hundred thirty	130
one hundred fifty	150
one hundred seventy-five	175
two hundred	200
five hundred sixty	560
one thousand	1,000
one thousand two hundred	1,200
two thousand	2,000

Prices

dollar	$
pound	£
euro	€
nine (pounds) (and) ninety-nine (pence)	£9.99
twenty-one (dollars) (and) ninety-five (cents)	$21.95
seventy-two (euros) (and) fifty (cents)	€72.50

VOCABULARY *EXTRA*

1 Put the name of a place in town from the list under the pictures.

bus station | parking garage | police station | skate park | theater

0 _____theater_____ 1 _____ 2 _____ 3 _____ 4 _____

2 Match the signs with the places from Exercise 1.

A _____
B _____
C _____
D _____
E _____

COME AND LIVE IN ...

CALGARY

Calgary is a city of 1.3 million people in Canada. It is next to two rivers and near the Rocky Mountains. It's a clean and friendly place to live. Calgary is usually warm, dry, and very sunny in the summer, but there is lots of snow in the winter. Many people who live in Calgary come from other Canadian cities and other countries. There are lots of places to see plays and hear live music. Country music is very popular. There are a lot of cafés and restaurants with food from all over the world. A lot of people like skiing, too. Near Calgary is the famous Banff National Park with beautiful Lake Louise. This fantastic park is in the Rocky Mountains.

MONTREAL

Montreal, in the province Quebec on the east coast, is Canada's second biggest city. Around 1.8 million people live here. French is the official language, but most people speak English, too. The city is on an island between the St. Lawrence and Ottawa rivers, close to the sea. Winter in Montreal is very cold (–20°C) and long. There is usually snow from December to March. Montreal has 35 kilometers of tunnels under the city. So, when it is cold, people can walk to stations, shopping centers, offices, banks, and many other buildings. The summer is short and warm, and there are some beautiful beaches near the city. There are a lot of exciting things to do in the city. You can eat in one of the excellent restaurants. In July, there is a big international jazz festival.

📖 READING

1 Read the text about two Canadian cities quickly. Which city is the biggest?

2 Read the texts again. Mark the sentences C (Calgary), M (Montreal), or B (both cities).

0 It's in Canada. `B`
1 It's near the mountains. ☐
2 It's on the coast. ☐
3 Two rivers pass the city. ☐
4 A lot of people speak two languages. ☐
5 It's very cold for four months or more. ☐
6 It's warm and dry a lot of the year. ☐
7 There are a lot of restaurants. ☐
8 Many people enjoy winter sports. ☐
9 There is an unusual travel system. ☐
10 People here like country music. ☐

3 **CRITICAL THINKING** Read what these people say. Are they in Calgary or Montreal? Write the name of the correct city.

1 The National Park is only 90 minutes by car. _____

2 The festival has people from all over the world. I love it! _____

3 We go to the beach after school sometimes. _____

4 Everyone here is very friendly. _____

5 It's cold outside, but I can walk to my office underground. _____

DEVELOPING *Writing*

Your town/city

1 `INPUT` **Read the text. Does Laurent like weekends in his town?**

A weekend in my town

I live in Béziers, in the south of France. I like my town. It isn't very big, but the people here are nice.

On the weekends, there are a lot of things to do. The town center is small, but there are some nice stores and cafés, so I go into the center on Saturday afternoon to meet my friends. We have lunch together, or we do some shopping. Some days, we don't buy anything, but it's always fun.

There's a movie theater in the town, too, so on Friday or Saturday nights, my friends and I see a movie together. I like volleyball, so on Sunday mornings, I play with a lot of friends at the park. There are three volleyball courts in the park. It's really good.

Not far from the town, there's a river. It's great to swim there, but only in the summer!

My town is OK, and my friends are great, so the weekends here are not bad.

2 `ANALYZE` **Complete the sentences with *or*, *and*, or *so*.**

1 On Saturday evenings, we go to the movie theater, _____ we see a movie.

2 Do you want to play soccer _____ volleyball?

3 My cousins live 300 kilometers away, _____ I don't visit them very often.

3 **Match the words (1–3) with the phrases (a–c).**

1 in   **a** the weekend
2 on   **b** the summer
3 on   **c** Sunday mornings

4 `PLAN` **Think about a weekend in your town/city. What do you do? Use the ideas below to make notes.**

What I do on Saturdays: _____
_____
What I do on Sundays: _____
_____
What I do with my friends: _____
_____
What we do in the summer: _____
_____
What we do in the winter: _____
_____

5 `PRODUCE` **Use your notes and the text about Béziers to write a text about weekends where you live. Write about 50 words.**

_____
_____
_____
_____
_____
_____
_____
_____
_____
_____
_____
_____
_____

✎ WRITING TIP: Connecting things

When writing your text, it's a good idea to use *and*, *or*, and *so* to join connected ideas together. For example:

We have a drink and a snack together, or we do some shopping.
I like volleyball, so on Sunday mornings I play with friends in the park.

🎧 LISTENING

1 🔊 4.02 **Listen to Stella and Max talking to their Aunt Mary. Check (✓) the places they talk about.**

> bank ☐ | bookstore ✓ | café ☐
> library ☐ | museum ☐ | park ☐
> pharmacy ☐ | post office ☐
> shopping center ☐ | station ☐
> supermarket ☐

2 🔊 4.02 **Listen again and correct the sentences.**

0 There isn't a good shopping center.
   There's a good shopping center.

1 The museum is on Grand Avenue.
   _____

2 The museum is very big.
   _____

3 The shopping center is next to the museum.
   _____

4 Max wants some pens and pencils for his project.
   _____

5 There aren't any cafés in the shopping center.
   _____

6 Aunt Mary's favorite café is next to the bookstore.
   _____

DIALOGUE

3 **Bea is in a clothes store. Put the conversation in order.**

☐ Woman $15.50.
☐ Woman   OK. That's $31.00, please.
☐ Woman   Hello. Can I help you?
☐ Woman   Yes. There's this one here.
☐ Bea   Hi. Yes. Do you have any yellow T-shirts?
☐ Bea   Great! I'd like two, please.
☐ Bea   Oh, it's really nice. How much is it?

4 **Complete the conversation with words and phrases from the list.**

> can | expensive | is | much | that's | three

Man 0 ___*Can*___ I help you?

Matteo Yes, do you have any postcards?

Man Yes, there are 1_____ different postcards.

Matteo How 2_____ are they?

Man They're $1.50 each.

Matteo OK, three, please.

Man That's $4.50.

Matteo And how much 3_____ that small book about the museum?

Man It's $5.70.

Matteo And that big book?

Man That's $25.00.

Matteo That's very 4_____ . Just the cards and the small book, please.

Man OK. 5_____ $10.20.

5 **Imagine you're in a bookstore. Write a conversation similar to the one in Exercise 3.**

_____
_____
_____
_____
_____
_____
_____
_____
_____
_____
_____
_____

Train to TH!NK

Exploring numbers

6 **Seth and Ari want to buy things for their room at home. They have $300. They buy five things, and they have $35 left. Check (✓) what they buy.**

armchair – $60 ☐
VR headset – $50 ☐
chair – $20 ☐
desk – $30 ☐
smart speaker – $25 ☐
table – $35 ☐
TV – $100 ☐

TOWARDS A2 Key for Schools

EXAM SKILLS: LISTENING
Identifying text type

1 🔊 4.03 **Listen to the three conversations. How many people are speaking in each conversation?**

Conversation 1: _____
Conversation 2: _____
Conversation 3: _____

2 **Match the descriptions with the pictures. Write 1–3 in the boxes.**

1 a news report on TV
2 an announcement at a train station
3 people in a shop

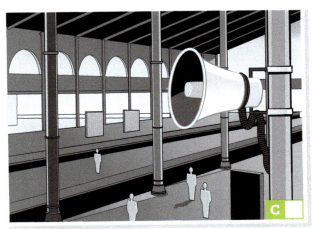

3 🔊 4.03 **Listen again. Match the situations with the pictures. Write A–C in the boxes.**

Conversation 1 ➜ picture ☐
Conversation 2 ➜ picture ☐
Conversation 3 ➜ picture ☐

🎧 LISTENING TIP

When you listen to a text for the first time, you don't need to understand every word. Listen to the important things:

* the number of speakers
* sounds and noises to tell you where the speakers are
* the way the speakers talk, e.g. are they happy, angry, worried, sad, excited, bored or none of these?
* 'important' words – read the question first and think of words (nouns, adjectives or verbs) that might help you to answer it. These are the 'important' words to listen for.

4 🔊 4.03 **Listen again to the three conversations. Which words in Exercise 3 helped you decide?**

Conversation 1: _____
Conversation 2: _____
Conversation 3: _____

CONSOLIDATION

🎧 LISTENING

1 🔊 **4.04** Listen to Joaquin talking about his family and where they live. Circle the correct answers (A, B, or C).

1 How many people are there in Joaquin's family?
- **A** six
- **B** eight
- **C** ten

2 How many sisters does Joaquin have?
- **A** four
- **B** five
- **C** six

3 Where is Joaquin from?
- **A** the US
- **B** France
- **C** Italy

4 What's his cousin's name?
- **A** Leo
- **B** Javi
- **C** Petra

2 🔊 **4.04** Listen again. How many are there? Write the numbers in the boxes.

 **A**

 **D**

 **B**

 **E**

 **C**

 **F**

🔤 VOCABULARY

3 Match the words in A with the words in B to make pairs.

A

> bathroom | brother | garage | husband
> kitchen | living room | son | uncle

B

> aunt | car | daughter | shower
> sister | sofa | wife

0 _bathroom – shower_
1 _____
2 _____
3 _____
4 _____
5 _____
6 _____
7 _____

4 Write the names of the shops and the prices.

0

pharmacy – It's three dollars and twenty-nine cents.

$3.29

1

_____
_____

$14.99

2

_____
_____

£2.50

3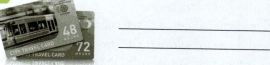

_____
_____

€79.59

4

_____
_____

£12.99

GRAMMAR

5 **Complete the sentences with words from the list. There are two extra words.**

> any | her | his | is | some | that | their | turn

1 Ask Luke. It's _____ sandwich.
2 There _____ a big park near my house.
3 Paul is Danny and Olivia's brother. He's _____ brother.
4 The shoe store? OK, just _____ right on Main Street and it's there.
5 There aren't _____ parks near here.
6 Can I see _____ dress in the window, please?

DIALOGUE

6 🔊 4.05 **Complete the conversation with words from the list. Then listen and check.**

> looks | much | really | right | thank | what

Jordan I like your T-shirt, Rachel.
Rachel ¹_____? It's very old.
Jordan Well, I think it ²_____ cool. And ³_____ a great hat, too.
Rachel ⁴_____ you. It's new.
Jordan How ⁵_____ was it?
Rachel Well, it was a present from my mom.
Jordan Oh, ⁶_____. I'll ask her, then.

READING

7 **Read the conversation and complete the sentences.**

Woman Hello, can I help you?
Junior Yes, I'd like to see those hats behind you.
Woman The black ones for teenagers?
Junior No, the red ones next to them.
Woman OK. Yes, these are really popular. Here you go.
Junior How much are they?
Woman Wait a minute. Let me see. They're $5.99.
Junior OK, great! Can I have three, please?
Woman Wow! You really like them.
Junior They're not for me. They're for my sisters.

Woman Your sisters?
Junior Yes, it's their birthday tomorrow. They're nine.
Woman So they're triplets?
Junior Yes, all three were born on the same day.
Woman Is it difficult? I mean, having three sisters?
Junior Three? There's three more as well.
Woman Six sisters? Poor you! Here, have a black hat. It's for you.
Junior Wow, thanks. That's really kind!

1 Junior wants to see the _____ hats.
2 The hats are _____ each.
3 The hats are for his _____.
4 It's their _____ tomorrow.
5 Triplets are _____ children born on the same day.
6 Junior has _____ sisters.
7 The woman gives Junior a free _____.
8 Junior thinks the woman is very _____.

WRITING

8 **Write a short text about your family and where you live. Write about 50 words. Use the questions to help you.**

• Who is in your family?
• What is your house like?
• What is your town like?

5 FREE TIME

GRAMMAR
Simple present

→ SB p.50

1 ★☆☆ **Circle** the correct options.

0 I (play) / plays tennis every day.
1 My cousins *speak* / *speaks* Spanish.
2 Mr. Clark *teach* / *teaches* history.
3 The dog *like* / *likes* the park.
4 We sometimes *go* / *goes* to bed very late.
5 You *live* / *lives* near me.

2 ★★☆ **Complete the sentences with the simple present form of the verbs in parentheses. Which four sentences match the pictures? Write the numbers in the boxes.**

0 My dad ____flies____ planes. (fly)
1 The boys _____ a lot of video games. (play)
2 Miss Dawson _____ technology. (teach)
3 Nina _____ in the library every day. (study)
4 Emily and Dana _____ the guitar. (play)
5 Mom _____ cats. (love)

 A
 C
 B
 D

3 ★★☆ **Complete the sentences with the correct form of the verbs in the list.**

> finish | go | like | play | speak
> study | teach | watch

0 Mom ____likes____ pop music.
1 My father _____ math at my school.
2 Lucia _____ to a drama club on Wednesdays.
3 Dennis _____ four languages. He's amazing.
4 My brother _____ TV after school.
5 Our school _____ at 3:15 p.m.
6 Jenna _____ the piano every afternoon.
7 My sister _____ every weekend.

PRONUNCIATION
Simple present verbs – third person
Go to page 119. 🎧

Adverbs of frequency

→ SB p.50

4 ★☆☆ **Put the adverbs in the correct order on the line.**

> often | always | sometimes | never

→

1 _____ 2 _____ 3 _____ 4 _____

5 ★★☆ **Write the sentences with the adverb of frequency in the correct place.**

0 I meet my friends in town on Saturdays. (sometimes)
I sometimes meet my friends in town on Saturdays.

1 Jennie is happy. (always)
_____

2 They do homework on the weekend. (never)
_____

3 You help Mom and Dad make dinner. (sometimes)
_____

4 We are tired on Friday evenings. (often)
_____

5 It rains on Sundays! (always)
_____

6 Mom flies to Miami for work. (often)
_____

7 I am bored on the weekends. (never)
_____

6 ⭐⭐⭐ **Write sentences so they are true for you. Use adverbs of frequency.**

1 do homework after school

_____

2 play computer games on the weekends

_____

3 watch TV on Sunday afternoons

_____

4 listen to music in the morning

_____

5 text my best friend in the evening

_____

Simple present (negative)   → SB p.51

7 ⭐⭐☆ **Complete the sentences with the negative form of the verbs in parentheses.**

0 My mom ___doesn't write___ books for children. (write)

1 I _____ music lessons after school. (have)

2 My cousins _____ to a lot of music. (listen)

3 My grandfather _____ model planes. (make)

4 We _____ games on our tablet. (play)

5 School _____ at 8:00 a.m. (start)

6 My sister _____ singing or dancing. (like)

7 You _____ in a small house. (live)

8 ⭐⭐☆ **Match these sentences with the sentences from Exercise 7.**

[0] She writes for teenagers.

a ☐ It's really big.

b ☐ But the gates open at that time.

c ☐ We play them on the computer.

d ☐ She's very shy.

e ☐ I have them on Saturdays.

f ☐ He makes trains.

g ☐ But they watch a lot of TV.

Simple present (questions)   → SB p.52

9 ⭐☆☆ **Complete the questions with Do or Does.**

0 ___Do___ you live in Sydney?

1 _____ Pablo like sports?

2 _____ you know the answer?

3 _____ your sister play tennis?

4 _____ you often go to the movies?

5 _____ your teacher give you a lot of homework?

10 ⭐⭐⭐ **Write the questions. Then write answers so they are true for you.**

0 your mother / speak English?

Does your mother speak English?
Yes, she does.

1 you / always do your homework?

_____

2 your best friend / play the piano?

_____

3 you / sometimes play computer games before school?

_____
_____

4 you and your friends / play basketball?

_____
_____

5 your mom / drive a big car?

_____
_____

GET IT RIGHT!

Adverbs of frequency

With the verb _to be_, we use this word order: subject + verb + adverb of frequency. With other verbs, we use this word order: subject + adverb of frequency + verb.

✓ He is always friendly.

✗ He always is friendly.

✓ I often watch soccer on TV.

✗ I watch often soccer on TV.

Circle the correct sentences.

0 a I eat often ice cream.

  b (I often eat ice cream.)

1 a I play often computer games.

  b I often play computer games.

2 a I always go to the movies with my friends.

  b Always I go to the movies with my friends.

3 a That singer is always great.

  b That singer always is great.

4 a I ride a bike in the park never.

  b I never ride a bike in the park.

5 a I sometimes am bored.

  b I am sometimes bored.

VOCABULARY
Free-time activities

1 ★☆☆ **Match the parts of the sentences.**

0 I play `e`
1 I go ☐
2 I hang out with ☐
3 I chat ☐
4 I listen ☐
5 I dance ☐

a shopping with Mom on Saturdays.
b with Suki online all the time.
c music in bed.
d to rock music with my friends.
e computer games on my tablet.
f my friends in the park after school.

2 ★★☆ **Complete the sentences with words from the list.**

> dance | homework | listens
> out | plays | shopping

0 Every day after school, I hang _____out_____ at the sports club.
1 Siena goes _____ with her sister on Saturday afternoons.
2 Tony never does his _____ on time.
3 We _____ every weekend at school dances.
4 My brother _____ computer games all weekend!
5 My dad _____ to really old music.

3 ★★★ **Write sentences that are true for you. Use adverbs of frequency.**

1 play computer games
_____

2 go shopping
_____

3 dance
_____

4 chat with friends online
_____

5 listen to music
_____

6 hang out with friends
_____

7 do homework
_____

8 go to the movies
_____

Gadgets

4 ★★☆ **Put the letters in order to make words for gadgets.**

0 blteat _____tablet_____
1 mnigag loscone _____
2 RV stheeda _____
3 marsthopen _____
4 ahehndspoe _____
5 SGP _____
6 plapto _____
7 ard-eere _____

5 ★★★ **Answer the questions so they are true for you.**

1 What do you use to play computer games?
_____

2 What do you use to listen to music?
_____

3 What do you use to not get lost?
_____

4 What do you use to read books, magazines, or comics?
_____

Days in your life

6 ★★☆ **Complete the days of the week with the missing letters. Then put the days in order.**

0 _M_ _o_ nday   **1** _____
1 __ __dnesday   **2** _____
2 __ __iday   **3** _____
3 __ __esday   **4** _____
4 __ __nday   **5** _____
5 __ __ursday   **6** _____
6 __ __turday   **7** _____

7 ★★★ **Choose three days. Write sentences so they are true for you.**

I love Fridays because I always go to the movies
with my dad in the evening.
_____
_____
_____
_____
_____
_____
_____
_____

REFERENCE
Free-time activities

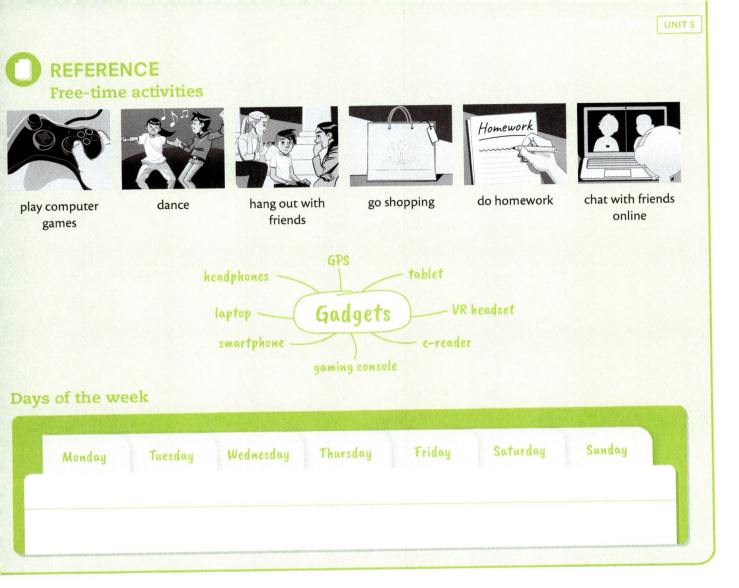

play computer games

dance

hang out with friends

go shopping

do homework

chat with friends online

headphones — GPS — tablet

laptop — Gadgets — VR headset

smartphone — e-reader

gaming console

Days of the week

Monday	Tuesday	Wednesday	Thursday	Friday	Saturday	Sunday

VOCABULARY *EXTRA*

1 Where do people usually do these activities? Check (✓) the correct column.

	indoors	outdoors
1 ride your bike	☐	☐
2 play board games	☐	☐
3 read comics	☐	☐
4 watch videos online	☐	☐
5 roller-skate	☐	☐

2 Complete the sentences so they are true for you. Use the activities from Exercise 1.

1 I often _____ after school.

2 I never _____ in the mornings.

3 I always _____ on the weekend.

4 I never _____ when I'm tired.

5 I sometimes _____ with my mom/dad.

3 Answer the questions about the activities from Exercise 1.

1 Which do you really like?

_____

2 Which do you often do?

_____

3 Which do you never do?

_____

Computer gaming club

Come and get better at all your favorite games. Learn from your friends and show them what you know. Mrs. Stephens also shows you how to make your own simple games.
A _____

Grades 7 and 8 – Tuesday at lunch in Room 4

Dance club

Join Mr. Roberts for an hour of exercise and have a lot of fun at the same time. Learn how to dance to all the best modern pop songs. And it's not just for students at the school – anyone is welcome!
C _____

All grades – Wednesdays at lunch in the school gym

MOVIE CLUB

Watch classic movies from the 1980s and 1990s: *E.T.*, *Toy Story*, *Jurassic Park*, etc. Then talk about them with Miss Owens and other students.
D _____

Bring your own popcorn!

Grades 9–11 – Thursday after school in Room 14

HOMEWORK CLUB

Don't do all of your homework after school or on the weekend. Come to Homework Club and do it all before you go home. There's always a teacher here to help you if you have a problem, so when you get home after school, you can have fun! B _____

All grades – every day after school in Room 8

📖 READING

1 **Look at the pictures and read the messages. Write the rooms and the names of the clubs.**

1 _____

3 _____

2 _____

4 _____

2 **Match the sentences or phrases with the correct places (A–D) in the messages.**

0 Tell your parents you finished your homework at 5 p.m. → **B**

1 Wear comfortable clothes! ▢

2 It's great for all students who love gadgets. ▢

3 Ask your parents about some of their favorites, and we can add them to the list. ▢

3 **CRITICAL THINKING** **Answer the questions. Write sentences.**

1 Which club do you like? Why?

_____
_____
_____

2 Which club don't you like? Why?

_____
_____
_____

3 Think of one more club to add. What can kids do there? When and where is it?

_____
_____
_____

DEVELOPING *Writing*

My week

1 **INPUT** **Read the text. On which day does Lucia not do any homework?**

Lucia's Busy Life

A typical week …

Posted: MONDAY, APRIL 10th

From Monday to Friday, I go to school from 9 a.m. to 3 p.m. every day. But my day doesn't finish then!

After school on Mondays, I have violin lessons from 4 p.m. to 5 p.m. In the evenings, I do my homework.

On Tuesdays and Thursdays, I go to karate class from 4 p.m. to 6 p.m. In the evenings, I do my homework.

On Wednesday afternoons, I go to gaming club from 3 p.m. to 4 p.m. And in the evenings? Yep, I do my homework.

On Fridays, I do my homework after school! I go to coding club in the evenings. It finishes at 9 p.m.

On Saturdays, I do things with Mom and Dad. We go shopping or visit Grandma. My dad sometimes takes us to watch soccer.

On Sundays, I sleep! Oh, and then I do some homework.

2 **ANALYZE** **Complete the sentences with the correct prepositions. Use the text in Exercise 1 to help you.**

1 I play tennis _____ Tuesdays and Thursdays. I play _____ 4 p.m. _____ 6 p.m.

2 _____ Wednesday afternoons, I go to dance club. It starts _____ 3 p.m. and finishes _____ 4 p.m.

3 _____ Monday to Friday, I go to school.

3 **Match the parts of the phrases. Then check your answers in the text in Exercise 1.**

1 do   a a piano lesson
2 go   b to dance club / shopping
3 have   c homework

4 **PLAN** **Think about your typical week. Use the questions to make notes.**

What do you do during the day? Which days are different?

_____

What do you do after school? What days do you do things on?

_____

What do you do in the evenings?

_____

What do you do on the weekend?

_____

✏ WRITING TIP: Prepositions

When you write about your week, be careful to use the correct preposition:

- *IN* the evening
- *ON* Monday evening / Saturday / the weekend
- *AT* night / 8 p.m.

5 **PRODUCE** **Use your notes and the sentences below to write a text about a typical week for you. Write about 50 words.**

_____
_____
_____
_____
_____
_____
_____
_____
_____
_____
_____

🎧 LISTENING

1 🔊 5.02 **Listen to Ashley and Robbie talking about a competition. Circle the correct option in each sentence.**

0 Ashley feels (worried) / excited about the competition.

1 She doesn't like *her team / people watching her.*

2 The competition is in *a museum / the robotics club.*

3 Robbie says Ashley forgets her *team / everything* else when she makes robots.

4 Robbie offers to come to the robotics club *with his friends / on his own.*

5 Ashley thinks this is *a good idea / not necessary.*

2 🔊 5.02 **Listen again and underline the incorrect information in the sentences. Then write the correct information.**

0 Ashley is in a <u>drama</u> competition.
robotics _____

1 Ashley doesn't like making robots.
_____

2 On the team, they don't work together.
_____

3 The competition is at the Natural History Museum.
_____

4 Robotics club is on Mondays and Wednesdays.
_____

5 Ashley doesn't want Robbie to come to robotics club.
_____

DIALOGUE

3 **Complete the conversation with the phrases from the list.**

> don't worry | here to help you | No problem
> You can do it | ~~you're good~~

Ashley ... And I don't like that.

Robbie Oh, I see. But your team is the best in our school, and ⁰___*you're good*___!

Ashley Hmm, do you think so?

Robbie Yes! So, come on. ¹_____ , Ashley.

Ashley Really?

Robbie Yes, of course! And I'm ²_____ .

Ashley You are? How?

Robbie Is the Robotics club on Thursday?

Ashley Yes, Monday and Thursday at lunchtime.

Robbie OK, so ³_____ ! Next time, I'm there with my friends to watch you!

Ashley Oh, thanks, Robbie. You're a really good friend!

Robbie ⁴_____ ! I want you to win.

4 **Look at the picture and write a short conversation. Use phrases from Exercise 3.**

PHRASES FOR FLUENCY → SB p.54

5 **Match the sentences.**

0 What's wrong? [d]

1 I have an idea. [ ]

2 Ana, do you want to be on the school soccer team? [ ]

3 I don't want to play soccer. [ ]

a Really. What is it?

b No way!

c Oh, come on. We really need you.

d I feel sick.

6 **Use two of the pairs of sentences in Exercise 5 to complete the conversations.**

Conversation 1

George _____

Sara _____

George But I hate soccer. And I'm terrible at it.

Sara No, you're not. You're great.

Conversation 2

Abi I'm sorry, Simon. I don't really want to go shopping.

Simon _____

Abi _____

Simon Oh, no. Let me get you a glass of water.

7 **Use the other two pairs of sentences in Exercise 5 to make your own conversations.**

SUM IT UP

1 This is Millie's diary. Make sentences about her week.

0 *On Monday, she goes to dance class.*

1 _____

2 _____

3 _____

4 _____

5 _____

Monday	dance class
Tuesday	roller-skating
Wednesday	shopping for comics
Thursday	computer games
Friday	friends
Saturday	music
Sunday	sleep

2 Use the code to work out the message.

CODE

● = a   ✳ = b   ▬▶ = c   ■ = d

✣ = e   ✿ = f   ✔ = g   ★ = h

✂ = i   ▶ = j   ◗ = k   ♣ = l

♥ = m   ☎ = n   ☞ = o   ➔ = p

♠ = q   ♦ = r   ❋ = s   ✺ = t

✎ = u   ○ = v   ✿ = w   ➤ = x

☆ = y   ❖ = z

3 What do you want for your birthday? Use the code to write your own message.

_____

_____

_____

6 BEST FRIENDS

→ 17 Grammar rap!

G GRAMMAR

have / has (positive and negative)

→ SB p.58

1 ★☆☆ **Circle** the correct options.

0 I *has* / *have* a new friend.
1 My friend Selena *has* / *have* a tablet.
2 Luna *has* / *have* a big family.
3 We *has* / *have* a cat.
4 All of my friends *has* / *have* bikes.

2 ★★☆ **Look at the table and complete the sentences with *have*, *has*, or *don't/doesn't have*.**

does / doesn't have	Sally	Tom	Dan	Mike
smartphone	✓	✗	✓	✗
laptop	✗	✗	✗	✗
bike	✓	✗	✓	✓
gaming console	✗	✓	✗	✗
cat	✓	✓	✓	✓

0 Tom ___*doesn't have*___ a smartphone.
1 Sally _____ a laptop or a gaming console.
2 Dan and Mike _____ a bike.
3 Tom _____ a gaming console.
4 All of them _____ a cat.
5 Tom and Dan _____ a laptop.

3 ★★★ **Write sentences so they are true for you. Use *have* or *don't have* and phrases from the list.**

> a big family | a pet | a new smartphone
> a sister | a tablet | black hair | brown eyes
> three brothers

1 _____
2 _____
3 _____
4 _____
5 _____
6 _____
7 _____
8 _____

4 ★★★ **Write sentences under the photos. Use phrases from the list and *have* or *has*.**

> a shaved head | long curly hair
> long straight hair | short curly hair

_____

_____

have / has (questions)

→ SB p.59

5 ★☆☆ **Circle** the correct options.

1 A *Do* / *Does* you have your own laptop?
  B No, I *don't* / *doesn't*. But my big brother has one.
2 A *Do* / *Does* Kate have a Little Mix poster?
  B No, she *don't* / *doesn't*. She doesn't like them.
3 A *Do* / *Does* Dario and Alexei have new gaming consoles?
  B No, they *don't* / *doesn't*. But I *have* / *has* one.
4 A *Do* / *Does* you have a lot of songs on your phone?
  B Yes, I *do* / *does*. I have thousands. I listen to them all the time.
5 A *Do* / *Does* you have bikes?
  B Yes, we *do* / *does*. We both have bikes. We ride to school every day.
6 A *Do* / *Does* Andrew have a sister?
  B No, he *don't* / *doesn't*. He has a brother.

6 ★★☆ **Complete the dialogue with the correct form of *have*.**

Amy ⁰ ___*Does*___ your mom ___*have*___ brown hair?

Marco No, she ¹_____ . She ²_____ black hair.

Amy ³_____ she _____ blue eyes?

Marco No, she ⁴_____ . She ⁵_____ green eyes.

Amy ⁶_____ she _____ a daughter?

Marco No, she ⁷_____ . She ⁸_____ . one son – me!

7 ★★★ **Complete the dialogue about a member of your family.**

Friend Does he/she have green eyes?

You ¹_____

Friend Does he/she have a big family?

You ²_____

Friend Does he/she have a car?

You ³_____

Friend Does he/she have a dog?

You ⁴_____

Friend Does he/she have a smartphone?

You ⁵_____

Countable and uncountable nouns

 → SB p.59

8 ★☆☆ **Write C (countable) or U (uncountable).**

0	chair	C
1	nose	
2	cat	
3	fun	
4	friend	

5	time	
6	work	
7	hospital	
8	name	
9	teacher	

9 Circle **the correct options.**

0 It's the weekend. Let's have *a* / *some* fun.

1 I have *a* / *some* sandwiches. I'm hungry. Let's eat one.

2 Let's listen to *a* / *some* music on your smartphone.

3 Marie has *a* / *some* red bike.

4 I have *a* / *some* money. Let's buy some ice cream.

5 He has *a* / *some* hobby – painting!

6 My dad has *a* / *some* work to do.

7 Miguel doesn't have *an* / *some* apple. He has *a* / *some* banana.

10 **Complete the dialogues with *a*, *an*, or *some*.**

1 A Would you like ___*some*___ ice cream?
  B No, thanks. I have _____ apple.

2 A Do you have _____ hobby?
  B Yes, I do. I sing in a band.

3 A Do you have _____ best friend?
  B Yes, I do. Her name's Zoey.

4 A I have _____ money from my mom.
  B Me, too!
  A That's good. Let's buy _____ cookies.

5 A I don't have a pen.
  B Oh, I have _____ pen. I have blue, black, and red. Is that OK?
  A Yes, perfect!

GET IT RIGHT!

Countable and uncountable nouns

We add *-s* to the end of countable nouns to make them plural, but not to uncountable nouns.

✓ *I have a lot of friends.*

✗ *I have a lot of friend.*

✓ *I drink a lot of water.*

✗ *I drink a lot of waters.*

Circle **the correct options.**

0 How many *pen* / *pens* does he have?

1 I listen to *musics* / *music* in my bedroom.

2 They have a lot of *hobby* / *hobbies*.

3 Do you have enough *money* / *moneys* for your lunch?

4 Homework isn't always a lot of *fun* / *funs*.

5 Her brother has two *phone* / *phones*.

6 This street has a lot of *store* / *stores*.

VOCABULARY
Parts of the body

→ SB p.58

1 ★☆☆ **Complete the sentences and the crossword with the same words.**

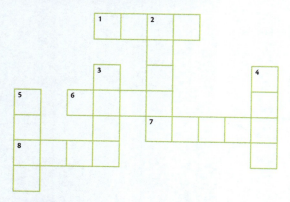

ACROSS

1 You hug with your _____ .

6 You kick with your _____ .

7 You hold with your _____ .

8 You hear with your _____ .

DOWN

2 You eat with your _____ .

3 You walk with your _____ .

4 You smell with your _____ .

5 You see with your _____ .

Describing people (1)

→ SB p.60

2 ★★☆ **Circle the correct options.**

0 His hair isn't curly. It's *wavy* / *brown*.

1 She has *short* / *blond* red hair.

2 Her eyes are *straight* / *green*.

3 My mother always wears her hair *straight* / *brown* for work.

4 The old man has gray *curly* / *hair*.

5 His hair *color* / *style* is black.

Describing people (2)

→ SB p.61

3 ★☆☆ **Complete the words with *a, e, i, o,* or *u*.**

0 m _u_ st _a_ ch _e_

1 gl __ ss __ s

2 t __ ll

3 b __ __ rd

4 sm __ l __

5 __ __ r r __ ngs

6 sh __ rt

4 ★☆☆ **Match the words with the things in the picture. Write 1–6 in the boxes.**

Seline | Mr. Chips | Arturo | Katy

1 beard | **2** earrings | **3** glasses
4 mustache | **5** wavy

5 ★★☆ **Look at the picture and write the names of the people.**

0 She has earrings. _Seline_

1 He has a very big mustache. _____

2 She has a lovely smile. _____

3 He has a very long beard. _____

4 She wears glasses. _____

6 ★★★ **Write one more sentence about each person from Exercise 4.**

1 _____

2 _____

3 _____

4 _____

PRONUNCIATION
Long vowel sound /eɪ/ Go to page 119.

REFERENCE

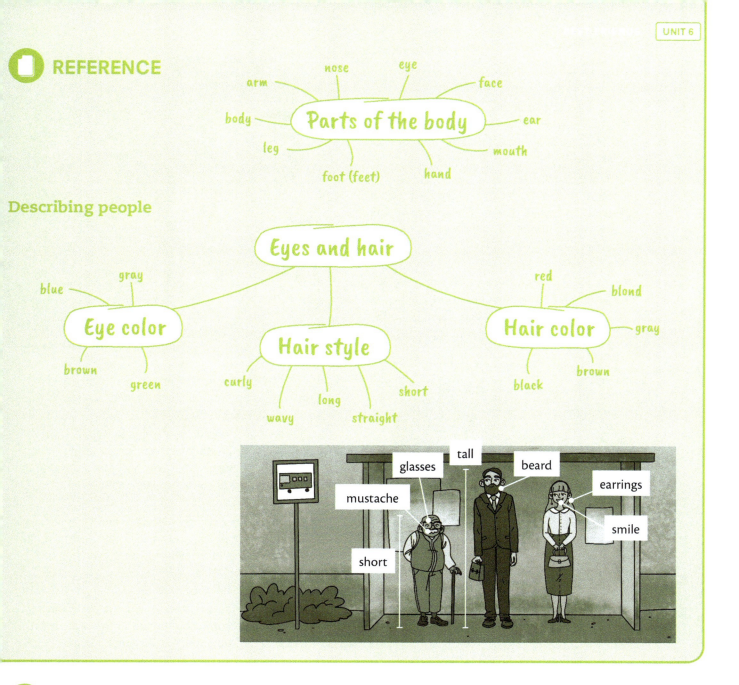

Parts of the body
- nose
- eye
- arm
- face
- body
- ear
- leg
- mouth
- foot (feet)
- hand

Describing people

Eyes and hair

Eye color
- blue
- gray
- brown
- green

Hair style
- curly
- wavy
- long
- straight
- short

Hair color
- red
- blond
- gray
- brown
- black

glasses · tall · beard · earrings · mustache · smile · short

VOCABULARY *EXTRA*

1 Match the words with the pictures.

1 braces | 2 braids | 3 ponytail | 4 old | 5 young

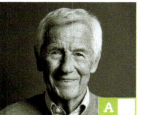 A

 B

 C

 D

 E

2 Circle the correct words.

1 A lot of teenagers have *braces / ponytail* on their teeth.

2 You're too *young / old* to go to college – you're only 16.

3 My brother has a *braids / ponytail*, but I don't like it.

4 My grandmother is very *young / old*, but she still plays a lot of sports.

5 People with long hair sometimes wear their hair in a ponytail or in *braids / braces*.

Q	Who is your best friend?
CLARA	My best friend's name is Keisha.
Q	What does she look like?
CLARA	She's very pretty. She has curly black hair and brown eyes. She wears glasses, and she has a friendly smile.
Q	What's she like?
CLARA	She's very smart, and she's very kind. She likes drawing and making things. I like making things, too. We have the same hobbies. I think that's really important.
Q	Why is she a good friend?
CLARA	Good friends share things with you. Keisha shares everything with me. She shares her chocolate and her clothes, too. She's a very special friend.

Q	Who is your best friend?
SAM	My best friend is a school friend named Miguel.
Q	What does he look like?
SAM	He's tall, and he has short straight brown hair and green eyes. He has a friendly smile, and he laughs a lot. We play video games together. We like the same things.
Q	What's he like?
SAM	He's funny and tells good jokes. He's very good at sports, and he likes basketball. I like basketball, too. We like the same team. That's important, I think.
Q	Why is he a good friend?
SAM	I think friends listen to you. Miguel always listens to me. Sometimes I have a problem, and he helps me. He's a great friend.

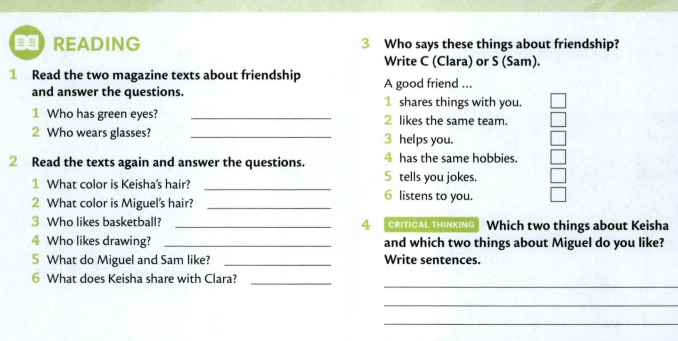

📖 READING

1 **Read the two magazine texts about friendship and answer the questions.**

  1 Who has green eyes? _____

  2 Who wears glasses? _____

2 **Read the texts again and answer the questions.**

  1 What color is Keisha's hair? _____

  2 What color is Miguel's hair? _____

  3 Who likes basketball? _____

  4 Who likes drawing? _____

  5 What do Miguel and Sam like? _____

  6 What does Keisha share with Clara? _____

3 **Who says these things about friendship? Write C (Clara) or S (Sam).**

A good friend ...

  1 shares things with you. ☐

  2 likes the same team. ☐

  3 helps you. ☐

  4 has the same hobbies. ☐

  5 tells you jokes. ☐

  6 listens to you. ☐

4 **CRITICAL THINKING** **Which two things about Keisha and which two things about Miguel do you like? Write sentences.**

_____

_____

_____

_____

DEVELOPING *Writing*

Describing people in a story

1 INPUT **Read about a singer from a story. What sports does he like?**

2 ANALYZE **Mark the sentences T (true) or F (false).**

1 He's short. ☐
2 He wears glasses. ☐
3 He's got a mustache. ☐
4 He doesn't have a beard. ☐
5 He doesn't like tennis. ☐

In my story, there's a singer. He's in a rock band. He's very tall. He has short black hair and green eyes, and he wears glasses. He has a short beard and a mustache. I think he's very good-looking. He's very active. He likes yoga and swimming, but he doesn't like tennis. He's very friendly. He has a big smile. I think he's cool.

3 PLAN **Think of a person from a story. He/She can be a singer, an athlete, an actor/actress, a prince/princess, etc. Choose the adjectives that describe him or her.**

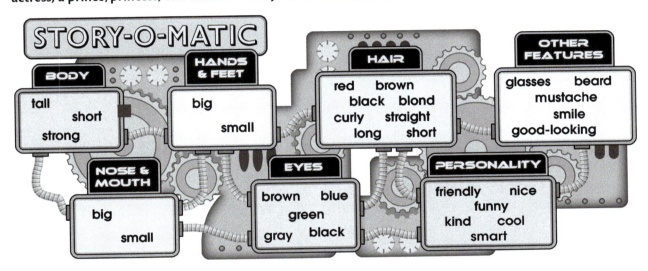

STORY-O-MATIC

BODY
tall
short
strong

HANDS & FEET
big
small

HAIR
red   brown
black   blond
curly   straight
long   short

OTHER FEATURES
glasses   beard
mustache
smile
good-looking

NOSE & MOUTH
big
small

EYES
brown   blue
green
gray   black

PERSONALITY
friendly   nice
funny
kind   cool
smart

4 **Write notes about your story person.**

What does he/she look like? (hair, eyes, other features): _____

_____

Personality: _____

_____

Likes/dislikes: _____

_____

WRITING TIP: Using adjectives to describe people

- He/She is *tall* / *short*.
- He/She has *long* / *black* / *curly* hair.
- He/She has *brown* / *blue* / *green* eyes.
- He/She has a *black* / *gray* / *brown* / *long* / *short mustache* / *beard*.
- He/She is *nice* / *friendly*.

5 PRODUCE **Use your notes and the model in Exercise 1 to write a text about your story person. Write about 50 words.**

_____

_____

_____

_____

_____

_____

 **LISTENING**

1 🔊 6.03 Listen to the conversations and number the places in the order you hear them.

a the park ☐

b a hospital ☐

c a party ☐

2 🔊 6.03 Listen again and (circle) the correct options.

1 Marco is *tall / short*, and he has short, curly *brown / black* hair. He has a *mustache / friendship band*, and he wears *glasses / earrings*.

2 Kenzie has a *dog / bike* with her. She's *short / tall*, and she has long, curly *brown / black* hair. She has *brown / blue* eyes, and she always wears *glasses / earrings*. She's very *funny / friendly*.

3 The nurse is *tall / short*, and she has *short / long* hair. It's *black / blond*, and it's *curly / straight*. She has *brown / green* eyes, and she's very *popular / pretty*.

DIALOGUE

3 Put the conversation in order.

☐ **Police officer** And what's your daughter's name?

☐ **Police officer** And what color eyes does she have?

1 **Police officer** Can I have your name?

☐ **Police officer** Thank you, Mr. Douglas.

☐ **Police officer** OK, first, what color hair does she have?

☐ **Police officer** Is it long or short?

☐ **Mr. Douglas** She has dark brown hair.

☐ **Mr. Douglas** My name's Neil Douglas.

☐ **Mr. Douglas** She has brown eyes, and she wears glasses.

☐ **Mr. Douglas** It's Ava.

☐ **Mr. Douglas** It's short and curly.

Train to TH!NK

Attention to detail

4 Find the five differences between Picture 1 and Picture 2 and write sentences.

Picture 1

Picture 2

0 *In picture 1, the woman has glasses.*
In picture 2, she doesn't have glasses.

1 _____

_____

2 _____

_____

3 _____

_____

4 _____

_____

EXAM SKILLS: WRITING
Punctuation (getting apostrophes right)

 WRITING TIP

When writing in English, it's sometimes easy to make mistakes with apostrophes ('). It's important to know when to use them and when not to use them.

- We use apostrophes to show missing letters in short forms, for example:

  He is ... ➡ *He's ...*

- Be careful not to confuse apostrophes for the short form of *be* with apostrophes to show possession:

  My mum's tall. (short form)

  My mum's name is Elena. (possession)

1 Complete the *Apostrophe Challenge*. Use contractions.

I think I can complete the *Apostrophe Challenge* in _____ seconds.

I am	**0** *I'm*
It is	**1**
You are	**2**
He is not	**3**
They are not	**4**
She has got	**5**
I have got	**6**
We have got	**7**
He has not got	**8**
I have not got	**9**

My time: _____ seconds.

2 Read the text. Put apostrophes in the correct places.

My best friends name is Leon. Hes 12 years old and hes in the same class as me. Leons got short, curly brown hair and green eyes. He wears glasses and hes very good-looking. Hes clever and he likes sports. Leons got a brother and a sister. Theyre eight years old and ten years old. Theyve got brown hair and blue eyes. They dont wear glasses. Leons also got a cat. Its black and white and its names Suky. Its a lovely cat.

3 Write a paragraph about one of these people. Use the questions in the box to help you.

a your best friend
b a family member
c your favourite actor/singer

- What's his/her name?
- How old is he/she?
- What does he/she look like?

_____

_____

_____

_____

_____

_____

_____

_____

CONSOLIDATION

🎧 LISTENING

1 🔊 6.04 **Listen to three conversations and (circle) the correct answers (A, B, or C).**

1 Jonathan has a problem with his …
   A arm.   **B** hand.   **C** leg.
2 Maddy is …
   A nice.   **B** short.   **C** tall.
3 How many friends does Diego have?
   A about fifty   **B** about fifteen   **C** about five

2 🔊 6.04 **Listen again and answer the questions.**

1 What does Jonathan want to do today?
   _____
2 What does the girl tell him to do?
   _____
3 Does Mike know Maddy?
   _____
4 What does Mike want Sofia to say to Maddy?
   _____
5 When does Diego come to this place?
   _____
6 What color is Jack's hair?
   _____

Ⓖ GRAMMAR

3 **Circle the correct options.**

Omar Hi, Joanna. How are you? It's nice to see a friend in town.

Joanna Hi, Omar. I ¹*come always / always come* here on Saturdays.

Omar Do you? ² *I'm never / I never am* in town on Saturdays, usually. But it's different today because ³*have / I have* some money from babysitting.

Joanna Great! ⁴*How much / How many* money do you have, then?

Omar $65. I ⁵*don't know / know not* what I want to buy, though. Maybe some clothes, or … .

Joanna That's a great idea. I love clothes. I ⁶*buy / buys* new clothes every month.

Omar Really? So, ⁷*you have / you has* a lot of clothes at home? Can you help me, then?

Joanna Sure! What do you need?

Omar Well, I'm not very good at buying clothes. Do you have ⁸*a / some* time to come with me?

Joanna Of course. It's fun! Let's go to that store first – ⁹*it always has / it has always* nice clothes.

Omar OK, cool. You know, Joanna, it's great to have ¹⁰*a / some* friend like you!

🔤 VOCABULARY

4 **Complete the sentences with the words in the list. There are two extra words.**

> do | earrings | eyes | hang out | headphones
> legs | short | smile | tall | VR headset

1 I really like listening to rap on the bus with my
   _____ .
2 Spiders have eight _____ .
3 I like Adela. She's always happy, and she has a nice
   _____ .
4 These are my new _____ . They're very long. Do you like them?
5 I love this _____ . It makes the games look more real.
6 She's good at basketball because she's very
   _____ .
7 I only _____ my homework on Sundays – never on Saturdays!
8 On Saturdays, I always _____ with my friends.

5 **Complete the words.**

1 My favorite day of the week is F_____ .
2 I use my t_____ every day to watch videos and play games.
3 His hair isn't straight. It's c_____ .
4 Let's go out on W_____ after school – to the park, maybe?
5 My dad has a b_____ and a mustache.
6 His eyes aren't very good. He wears g_____ all the time.
7 Do you want to go s_____ in town tomorrow afternoon?
8 Don't shout! Raise your h_____ if you know the answer.

DIALOGUE

6 🔊 **6.05** **Complete the dialogue with words from the list. Then listen and check.**

> always | an idea | computer | don't have | listen to | never | on | play | way | wrong

Pablo Hey, Kylie. You don't seem very happy. What's ¹_____?

Kylie Hi, Pablo. I'm OK. It's nothing.

Pablo Come ²_____. Is there a problem? Tell me.

Kylie No, not really. I want to ³_____ board games tonight, but I ⁴_____ anyone to play with.

Pablo OK. Listen. I have ⁵_____. Let's ask Jon to come over to my house. Then we can all play some games together.

Kylie No ⁶_____! I don't like Jon at all. He ⁷_____ helps me or says anything nice to me. He's ⁸_____ horrible to me.

Pablo Oh, right. Then it's you and me. Two people are enough for some games.

Kylie Yes. That's true. Thanks, Pablo. So – what games do you have?

Pablo Me? Sorry, Kylie, I don't have any board games. But I have some ⁹_____ games. Is that OK?

Kylie No, I don't really like them! But don't worry. I can bring one or two of my board games. And we can ¹⁰_____ music at the same time, too. You have music, don't you?

Pablo Of course! On my phone! See you later!

📖 READING

7 **Read this text about gadgets and (circle) the correct answers (A or B).**

Me and my gadgets

I'm Zack. I'm a 13-year-old boy … and I love my gadgets. I have a tablet, a smartphone, and an e-reader, and I'm always looking at one of them.

I use my tablet at home to read sports news and chat with my friends.

I use my smartphone … well, of course, make phone calls and send text messages. It's good, too, when I'm on the bus. I always use it listen to music. I have a lot of apps, too – especially music and sports apps, because they're my favorite free-time activities.

And my e-reader? I use it to read books. I love reading, and my parents and other people in my family often give me e-books to read (like for my birthday). I like reading before I go to sleep. I often read 20 or 30 pages at night.

1 Zack has …
  A three gadgets.
  B four gadgets.
2 He listens to music on …
  A his smartphone.
  B his tablet.
3 Zack uses his smartphone to …
  A read about the news and weather.
  B talk to his friends.
4 People in Zack's family often give him …
  A e-books for his reader.
  B pages from books to read at night.

✏️ WRITING

8 **Write a paragraph about your gadgets. Write about 50 words. Use the questions to help you.**

- What gadgets do you have?
- What do you use them for?
- When/How often do you use them?
- What gadgets do you want?

7 LIVING FOR SPORTS

Grammar rap!
▶20

ⓖ GRAMMAR
can (ability)

→ SB p.68

1 ★☆☆ **Match the sentences with the pictures. Write 1–8 in the boxes.**

1 He can ride a bike.
2 They can sing.
3 They can swim.
4 We can dance.
5 We can't dance.
6 He can't swim.
7 They can't sing.
8 He can't ride a bike.

A

E

B

F

C

G

D

H

2 ★★☆ **Match the questions and answers.**

0 Can you and Jayden sing?   e
1 Can you speak Italian?   ☐
2 Can David play the violin?   ☐
3 Can Helen cook?   ☐
4 Can a Ferrari go fast?   ☐
5 Can Karim and Jake ride a bike?   ☐

a No, he can't.
b Yes, they can.
c Yes, I can.
d Yes, it can.
e No, we can't.
f Yes, she can.

3 ★★★ **Write sentences with *can* and *can't*.**

0 I / ride a bike (✓) / roller-skate (✗)
   I can ride a bike, but I can't roller-skate.

1 I / sing (✓) / dance (✗)
   _____

2 my little sister / talk (✗) / walk (✓)
   _____

3 they / speak Spanish (✓) / speak Turkish (✗)
   _____

4 my brother / drive (✗) / cook (✓)
   _____

5 we / jump high (✗) / run fast (✓)
   _____

6 my grandmother / play the piano (✗) /
   play the guitar (✓)
   _____

7 birds / sing (✓) / talk (✗)
   _____

PRONUNCIATION
Vowel sound /ɔr/ Go to page 120.

4 ★★★ **Look at the pictures and write questions with *can*. Then answer them so they are true for you.**

0 *Can you drive?*
No, I can't.

1 _____
_____

2 _____
_____

3 _____
_____

4 _____
_____

5 ★★★ **Complete the sentences with your own ideas.**

1 I can't _____ ,
but I can _____ .

2 My best friend can _____ ,
but he/she can't _____ .

3 My teacher can't _____ ,
but he/she can _____ .

4 Babies can _____ ,
but they can't _____ .

5 My mom can _____ ,
but she can't _____ .

6 My dad can't _____ ,
but he can _____ .

7 The cat can _____ ,
but it can't _____ .

Prepositions of time

→ SB p.71

6 ★☆☆ **Circle the correct options.**

0 I leave home *at* / *in* / *on* 7 a.m. to go to school.

1 Julieta's birthday is *at* / *in* / *on* May.

2 The game starts *at* / *in* / *on* 8 p.m.

3 It's very hot *at* / *in* / *on* the summer.

4 I don't go to school *at* / *in* / *on* Sundays.

5 There's a holiday *at* / *in* / *on* April 7th this year.

6 We play volleyball *at* / *in* / *on* Friday afternoons.

7 The first day of school is *at* / *in* / *on* the fall.

7 ★★☆ **Complete the sentences with *at*, *in*, or *on*.**

0 The party is on Saturday ____*at*____ 7 p.m.

1 School starts _____ 8 a.m., and it finishes _____ 3 p.m.

2 It's not very cold _____ the spring.

3 My school break starts _____ June and finishes _____ September.

4 My birthday is _____ April 1st.
It's _____ the spring. This year it's _____ a Monday.

8 ★★☆ **Write the words in the correct columns.**

Friday | May | May 22nd | midnight
night | noon | September | seven o'clock
the evening | the morning | Tuesday
3:30 p.m. | July 7th

in	on	at
May		

GET IT *RIGHT!*

Prepositions of time

We use *on* for days of the week and dates.

✓ *I go swimming on Saturday.*

✗ *I go swimming in Saturday.*

✓ *Her birthday is on May 1st.*

✗ *Her birthday is in May 1st.*

We use *at* for clock times.

✓ *My dance lesson is at five o'clock.*

✗ *My dance lesson is on five o'clock.*

We use *in* for months and seasons.

✓ *Is your birthday in November?*

✗ *Is your birthday at November?*

✓ *We often go to the beach in the summer.*

✗ *We often go to the beach at the summer.*

Complete the sentences with *at*, *in*, or *on*.

0 I will be there ____*on*____ Sunday evening.

1 He wants to have a party _____ July 7th.

2 I can come _____ Monday or Friday.

3 My school exams are _____ June.

4 Can you meet me _____ ten thirty?

5 The trees are pretty _____ the fall.

6 It starts _____ a quarter to eight.

VOCABULARY
Sports

→ SB p.68

1 ★★★ Look at the pictures and write sentences.

Carlo   Lewis   Megan   Adam

Liz   Ethan   Amelia   Marta

0 ____Carlo skis.____
1 _____
2 _____
3 _____

4 _____
5 _____
6 _____
7 _____

Telling the time

→ SB p.69

2 ★★☆ Write the times under the clocks.

0 ____It's seven o'clock.____
3 _____

1 _____
4 _____

2 _____
5 _____

Months and seasons

→ SB p.71

3 ★★☆ Complete the months and seasons with the missing consonants.

Months
1 O _ _ o _ e _
2 _ u _ e
3 A _ _ i _
4 _ e _ e _ _ e _
5 _ a _
6 _ u _ _
7 _ a _ u a _ _
8 A u _ u _ _

9 _ e _ _ e _ _ e _
10 _ o _ e _ _ e _
11 _ e _ _ u a _ _
12 _ a _ _ _ _

Seasons
13 _ u _ _ e _
14 f _ l _
15 _ _ _ i _ _
16 _ i _ _ e _

4 ★★★ Choose four months. Say what season they are in and what you do in each month.

0 _August is in the summer. I go on vacation with my_
  family in August.
1 _____
  _____
  _____
2 _____
  _____
  _____
3 _____
  _____
4 _____
  _____
  _____

Ordinal numbers

→ SB p.71

5 ★☆☆ Complete the table.

1st	first	9th	
	second	10th	
3rd			eleventh
4th		12th	
	fifth		thirteenth
6th		20th	
7th		30th	
8th			thirty-first

6 ★★☆ Write the ordinal numbers.

0 14th ____fourteenth____
1 21st _____
2 27th _____
3 22nd _____
4 28th _____
5 15th _____
6 16th _____
7 23rd _____
8 29th _____
9 24th _____
10 17th _____
11 18th _____
12 19th _____
13 26th _____
14 25th _____

REFERENCE

Sports
- play basketball
- dive
- cycle
- ski
- skateboard
- do gymnastics
- do Taekwondo
- play volleyball

Months
- November
- December
- January
- October
- February
- September
- March
- August
- April
- July
- June
- May

Ordinal numbers

1st – first	5th – fifth	9th – ninth	13th – thirteenth
2nd – second	6th – sixth	10th – tenth	20th – twentieth
3rd – third	7th – seventh	11th – eleventh	30th – thirtieth
4th – fourth	8th – eighth	12th – twelfth	31st – thirty-first

Telling the time

1 It's three o'clock.

2 It's eight thirty.

3 It's a quarter after ten.

4 It's a quarter to one.

Seasons
- winter
- spring
- fall
- summer

VOCABULARY *EXTRA*

1 Match the objects in the pictures with the sports from the list.

badminton | foosball | frisbee | karate | netball | running

1 _____ 2 _____ 3 _____ 4 _____ 5 _____ 6 _____

2 Complete the sentences with the correct sport from Exercise 1.

1 We often play _____ at the café near my house.
2 Girls at my school play _____ . It's a little like basketball.
3 To go _____ , all you need is a pair of sneakers.
4 When you play _____ , you use a racket, but not a ball.
5 I do _____ , a Japanese martial art.
6 A lot of people play _____ in the park.

SPORTS
FOR ALL

The Paralympic Games are a big sporting event for athletes with disabilities. The Games show the world all the amazing things that these athletes can do. They take place every two years: after the Summer Olympics and after the Winter Olympics. Here are two incredible Paralympians.

This is ³_____ .
He's from ⁴_____ .

Jessica Long is American. Jessica has no legs below the knee, but she's a fantastic swimmer. She can swim really fast using only her arms and body. She's a very successful Paralympian. She has a lot of gold medals from several different Paralympic Games! Jessica loves sports and also plays basketball and goes ice-skating, cycling, and rock-climbing. Another interesting fact about Jessica is her birthday. It's February 29th – this happens only every four years!

Jaryd Clifford is Australian. He can't see very well, but he can run really fast. He can run 1,500 meters in 3 minutes and 47 seconds – that's in the top ten for *all* athletes in Australia! Because he can't see, Jaryd runs with a guide. His name is Tim Logan, and he's a good runner, too. Tim can see, so he helps Jaryd stay on the track and tells Jaryd where the other runners are. Tim is also Jaryd's friend and knows him well, so they are a good team. Jaryd is young, but he's already very successful. He has a lot of medals, including a gold one and a world record. He wants to get even better in the future!

This is ¹_____ .
She's from ²_____ .

📖 READING

1 **Read the text and complete the sentences under the pictures.**

2 **Read the text again and answer the questions.**
1 When do the Paralympics happen? _____
2 How does Jessica swim? _____
3 Does Jessica have medals from more than one Paralympics? _____
4 What is different about Jessica's birthday? _____
_____
5 What can't Jaryd Clifford do? _____
6 How does he stay on the track? _____
7 Why are Jaryd and Tim a good team? _____
_____

3 **CRITICAL THINKING** **Read the information about the athletes. Is each sentence about Jessica (JL) or Jaryd (JC)?**
1 _____ can win races with athletes who don't have disabilities.
2 _____ spends a lot of time doing different sports.
3 _____ has a lot of gold medals from many different Paralympic Games.
4 A good friend helps _____ to be an amazing athlete.
5 _____ doesn't have a birthday every year.
6 _____ has a world record.

DEVELOPING *Writing*

An amazing person

1 **INPUT** **Read the text. What sport is mentioned?**

MY AMAZING GRANDMA

My grandma Ana is an amazing person. We live in the same city, San Diego, so I see her a lot. She's 72 years old, and she still swims every day. She's on a team at a swimming club and does races most weekends. She swims in special races for people over 65. She always wins. She's really fast. She can swim 400 meters in five minutes. She loves swimming. It makes her feel young. I like her because she's a great swimmer, she's fun, and she makes really good cookies!

2 **ANALYZE** **Imagine you're the writer of the text and answer the questions.**

0 Who is she?
My grandma Ana.

1 Where does she live?
_____

2 What does she do?
_____

3 What amazing things can she do?
_____

4 Why do you like her?
_____

3 **PLAN** **Make notes about an amazing person you know.**

1 Who is he/she?
_____

2 Where does he/she live?
_____

3 How old is he/she?
_____

4 What amazing things can he/she do?
_____

5 Why do you like him/her?
_____

WRITING TIP: Third person "s" for *he, she,* and *it*

In English it's easy to forget the "s" at the end of verbs in the third person singular!

She swims every day.

She does races.

It makes her feel young.

4 **PRODUCE** **Use your answers to the questions in Exercise 3 to write a short text about your person. Write about 60 words.**

_____
_____
_____
_____
_____
_____
_____
_____
_____
_____
_____
_____

LISTENING

1 🔊 7.03 **Listen and match the conversations with the pictures. Write 1–3 in the boxes.**

A [ ]

B [ ]

C [ ]

2 🔊 7.03 **Listen again and draw the times on the clocks.**

Conversation 1:
What time do they play tennis?

Conversation 2:
What time is the movie they choose?

Conversation 3:
What time do they meet?

3 🔊 7.03 **Listen again and complete each sentence with one word.**

0 Louise feels a little _____bored_____ .

1 Louise is _____ until 1 p.m.

2 Rosie wants to go to the movies in the _____ .

3 The first movie is at _____ thirty.

4 Lucy wants to go _____ with Dan.

5 Lucy finishes _____ at five.

DIALOGUE

4 **Put the conversation in order.**

[ ]	Ben	We can't. We don't have a frisbee.
[ ]	Ben	Videos! That's why I'm bored. I'm tired of watching videos.
[ ]	Ben	We can't. She's on vacation.
[1]	Ben	I'm bored. What can we do?
[ ]	Selma	Is she? So how about some more videos?
[ ]	Selma	Why don't we play frisbee?
[ ]	Selma	No frisbee? OK, let's go to Eva's house.

PHRASES FOR FLUENCY → SB p.72

5 **Match the questions with the answers.**

0 Are these your things? [c]

1 Oh, no, look at the rain. [ ]

2 Where's Cape Town? [ ]

3 Look, there goes the bus. <u>Now what</u>? [ ]

a <u>It's no big deal</u>. I have an umbrella.

b <u>I'm sure</u> it's in South Africa.

c No, I think that's Dean's <u>stuff</u>.

d Don't worry. There's another one in 15 minutes.

6 **Complete the dialogue with the words and phrases that are underlined in Exercise 5.**

Mom   Come on, Owen. It's time for school.

Owen   I'm ready, Mom.

Mom   Do you have your swimming ⁰_____stuff_____ ?

Owen   I don't have a swimming lesson today.

Mom   ¹_____ you do, Owen. It's Thursday.

Owen   Thursday! Oh, no. I have a swimming lesson! But my towel's wet. ²_____ ?

Mom   ³_____ . You can take another towel.

Owen   Thanks, Mom. You're the best!

SUM IT UP

1 Read and write the names of the sports.

Welcome to a day of **sports** on B C B TV.

We've got a great show of sports action for you this Saturday.

We have live 0 ___*soccer*___ from Anfield, where Liverpool plays Manchester City in the big game.

We have 1 _____ with ALL the action from the NBA.

There's 2 _____ from last night's game between Brazil and China.

There's live 3 _____ from the World Championships in Copenhagen.

And we have 4 _____ from the Alpine World Cup, this weekend in Croatia.

There's something for everyone!

2 Read the clues and complete the TV sports programs.

Start time	Finish time	Sports program
1 p.m.	*1:30 p.m.*	
p.m.	p.m.	
p.m.	p.m.	
p.m.	p.m.	
p.m.	p.m.	

1 The afternoon of sports starts at 1 p.m.
2 Gymnastics is the fourth program.
3 The skiing is on for half an hour.
4 Soccer is after volleyball.
5 Basketball starts six hours after skiing finishes.
6 The soccer starts at 3 p.m.

7 Gymnastics is on for two and a half hours.
8 Volleyball is on for an hour and a half.
9 There are eight hours of sports.
10 Skiing is the first sport.
11 The last show is 90 minutes long.

3 Put the words in the list into four categories. There are three words in each category. Name the categories.

August | cycling | fifth | first | June | May | snowboarding | spring | summer | Taekwondo | third | winter

1 MONTHS	2	3	4
August			

8 FEEL THE RHYTHM

Grammar rap!
▶ 23

GRAMMAR
Present continuous

→ SB p.76

1 ★☆☆ **Circle the correct options.**

0 She isn't here. She **'s** / 're skateboarding in the park.

1 What *is* / *are* you doing?

2 Sorry, I can't talk now. I **'m** / *is* watching a movie.

3 All my friends are here. We **'s** / **'re** having a great time!

4 My brother's in his room. He **'s** / **'re** playing computer games.

5 My mom and dad *is* / *are* shopping at the supermarket.

6 I think they're happy. They **'s** / **'re** smiling a lot!

7 Look! There's Zack. Where **'s** / **'re** he going?

2 ★☆☆ **Write the *-ing* form of these verbs.**

0 shop _____*shopping*_____

1 play _____

2 give _____

3 sit _____

4 dance _____

5 smile _____

6 run _____

7 walk _____

8 read _____

9 take _____

10 try _____

11 stop _____

12 write _____

13 draw _____

3 ★★☆ **Complete the sentences with the present continuous form of the verbs in parentheses.**

0 Go away, Li. I ____*'m not talking*____ to you! (not talk)

1 Let's go for a walk. It _____ . (not rain)

2 _____ you _____ the party? (enjoy)

3 _____ your brother _____ a good time in college? (have)

4 What _____ you _____ , Joaquim? (do)

5 The TV is on, but they _____ it. (not watch)

6 Ivy! You _____ to me! (not listen)

7 What _____ the cat _____ ? (eat)

8 They _____ well today. (not play)

4 ★★☆ **Lily is telling Juan about a new game show on TV. Complete the conversation with the present continuous form of the verbs in parentheses.**

Lily Hey, Juan, how are you? Are you free this evening?

Juan Hmm, I'm not sure. Why?

Lily Well, there's a great new game show on TV. There are two teams. When it starts, a player on one team **0**____*is watching*____ (watch) a video on a tablet. Of course, the other players can't see what **1**_____ (happen) on the screen.

Juan So?

Lily Well, the player with the tablet says things like, "A boy **2**_____ (run). He **3**_____ (wear) shorts. He **4**_____ (hold) a ball." After each sentence, the other players guess what **5**_____ (happen) in the video.

Juan And then what?

Lily The players can ask ten questions.

Juan Like, "What **6**_____ they _____ (do) in the video?"

Lily No, of course not. They can only ask questions like, "**7**_____ the boy _____ (play) with friends?" or "**8**_____ they _____ (go) to school?" or "**9**_____ they _____ (watch) a game of soccer?"

Juan And then?

Lily Sometimes the player watching the video says what **10**_____ (not happen) in the video. Things like, "The boy **11**_____ (not sitting) on the floor," or "The people **12**_____ (not play) music." And the other player gets a point if they can say what's happening in the video.

Juan Hmm. I don't like watching game shows. I like watching movies.

Lily Oh. Well, please watch tonight. There's a surprise for you!

Juan A surprise? For me? Now I want to watch it!

5 ★★★ Complete this extract from the game show with the correct form of the verbs in the list.

> hit | hold | kick | not go | not smile
> not throw | play (x3) | stand | wear

Host Let's play! Lily, you have the tablet, so your team starts.

Lily Well, I can see 12 girls here. They ⁰ _'re wearing_ shorts and T-shirts.

Simon ¹ _____ they _____ a game?

Lily Yes, they are. They ² _____ with a ball.

Keiko ³ _____ they _____ the ball with their feet?

Lily No, they aren't. And they ⁴ _____ the ball. One girl ⁵ _____ the ball in her hand. She ⁶ _____ behind a line on the floor.

Paulo ⁷ _____ she _____ the ball with her hand?

Lily Yes, she is. But the ball ⁸ _____ into the net. That's not good. She isn't happy. She ⁹ _____ .

Keiko I know! ¹⁰ _____ they _____ volleyball?

Lily Yes, they are!

Host Great job! That's one point to you.

6 ★★★ What do you think your family and friends are doing now? Look at the example and write similar sentences about them.

0 _I think my sister is reading a magazine now._
1 _____
2 _____
3 _____
4 _____
5 _____

like / don't like + -ing

→ SB p.78

7 ★★☆ Write sentences with the correct form of the verbs.

0 I / like / read / long books
I like reading long books.

1 my sister / not like / do / gymnastics
_____

2 my parents / hate / watch / scary movies
_____

3 my best friend / like / listen to / classical music
_____

4 I / not like / go to / buy clothes
_____

5 I / love / read / in bed
_____

8 ★★☆ Complete the text. Use *love* (😃😃), *like* (😃), *don't/doesn't like* (☹), *hate* (☹☹), and the correct form of the verbs.

> My family is a little strange – they like or don't like all kinds of different things. My sister
> ⁰ _doesn't like cooking_ (☹ cook), but she
> ¹ _____ (😃😃 clean) her room.
> My father ² _____ (☹☹ go) for walks, but he ³ _____ (😃 take) exercise classes at the gym. My mother
> ⁴ _____ (😃 read) books, but she
> ⁵ _____ (☹☹ look) at magazines.
> My parents ⁶ _____ (😃😃 travel) to other countries, but they ⁷ _____ (☹ speak) other languages. And me? Well, I just
> ⁸ _____ (😃😃 be) with my strange family!

9 ★★☆ Complete the sentences so they are true for you.

0 I love ___ _singing in the shower_ ___ and ___ _dancing in my bedroom_ ___ .

1 I love _____ and _____ .

2 I like _____ and _____ .

3 I don't like _____ and _____ .

4 I hate _____ and _____ .

GET IT RIGHT!

Present continuous

We use subject + *am/is/are* + *-ing* form of the main verb.

✓ *We are watching a video.*
✗ *We watching a video.*
✓ *I am eating a sandwich.*
✗ *I am eat a sandwich.*

Complete the sentences with the correct present continuous form of the verbs in parentheses.

0 She ___ _is taking_ ___ (take) some photos of her food.

1 We _____ (do) the shopping at the moment.

2 _____ (you / listen) to rap music?

3 He _____ (wear) a red shirt and black pants.

4 They _____ (walk) to the sports center.

5 Who _____ (play) computer games?

6 He _____ (not eat) a sandwich; he's eating cake!

VOCABULARY
Present continuous verbs

→ SB p.76

1 ⭐☆☆ **Look at the picture above and complete the sentences with the correct form of the verbs from the list.**

> cheer | dance | leave | read | run | sing
> sit | smile | stand | take | talk | wear

0 Pierre is ___running___ .

1 Elena is _____ .

2 Charlie is _____ .

3 Lucy is _____ on a bench.

4 Lucas and Kerry are _____ .

5 Callum is _____ a hat.

6 Helena is _____ .

7 Rob is _____ .

8 Claire is _____ on her phone.

9 Matt is _____ a photo.

10 Fiona is _____ .

11 Jen and Pablo are _____ the park.

2 ⭐⭐☆ **Complete each sentence with a verb from Exercise 1. Use the correct form of the verbs.**

0 I'm ___reading___ a really good book. It's very interesting!

1 My dad's crazy. He wants to _____ a marathon.

2 Let's _____ a song.

3 This train _____ at 10:45 and arrives in Atlanta at 12:40.

4 Look at Mike! He's _____ green pants and a purple sweater!

5 Can you _____ a photo of us, please?

6 I love _____ on the phone with my friends.

7 This is my favorite chair. I love _____ here.

Clothes

→ SB p.79

3 ⭐⭐☆ **Find 11 more clothes items in the word search.**

P	R	O	U	D	E	D	J	A	N	S	T
A	S	H	I	R	T	R	A	S	E	H	P
N	A	T	H	L	O	E	W	K	S	I	O
T	R	E	A	I	N	S	X	C	R	R	R
S	N	A	E	J	O	S	H	O	E	S	E
H	T	L	O	T	S	A	U	S	S	W	T
E	R	B	K	R	H	B	N	Y	B	E	A
R	I	R	W	E	O	U	K	J	P	A	E
L	H	A	D	I	R	Y	L	U	R	F	W
P	S	C	O	A	T	T	R	N	Z	E	S
J	T	R	I	K	S	G	E	S	A	R	M
U	M	B	E	S	R	E	K	A	E	N	S

4 ⭐⭐☆ **Circle the odd one out in each list.**

0 jeans   sweater   shirt

1 socks   sneakers   coat

2 shorts   T-shirt   pants

3 dress   skirt   shoes

4 sweater   T-shirt   coat

5 ⭐⭐⭐ **Write answers to the questions so they are true for you.**

1 What clothes do you love wearing on the weekend?

_____

2 What clothes do you never buy?

_____

3 Of all the people you know, who wears really nice clothes? What do they wear?

_____

PRONUNCIATION
Intonation – listing items Go to page 120. 🎧

REFERENCE
Verbs

base form	-ing form
cheer	cheering
dance	dancing
leave	leaving
read	reading
run	running
sing	singing
sit	sitting
smile	smiling
stand	standing
take	taking
talk	talking
wear	wearing

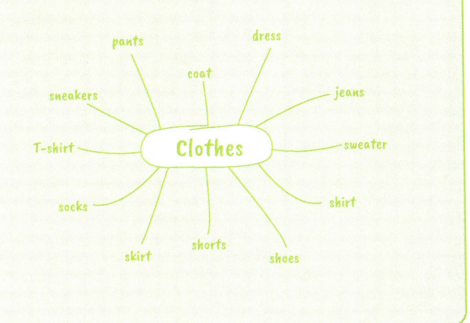

Clothes — pants, dress, coat, sneakers, jeans, T-shirt, sweater, socks, shirt, skirt, shorts, shoes

VOCABULARY *EXTRA*

1 **Label the picture with the words from the list of clothes.**

handbag | necklace | raincoat | suit | tie | umbrella

3 _____
4 _____
2 _____
5 _____
1 _____
6 _____

2 **Complete the sentences with words from the list in Exercise 1.**

1 Our school uniform has black pants, a white shirt, and a red _____ .

2 It's raining! You need to wear your _____ and take an _____ .

3 Gio's dad doesn't want to wear a _____ every day to work. He likes jeans and T-shirts!

4 "That's a beautiful _____ ."
   "It's a birthday present for my sister. It's gold."

5 "Oh, no! I can't find my _____ . My new phone's in it."
   "Don't worry, Mom. It's on the sofa."

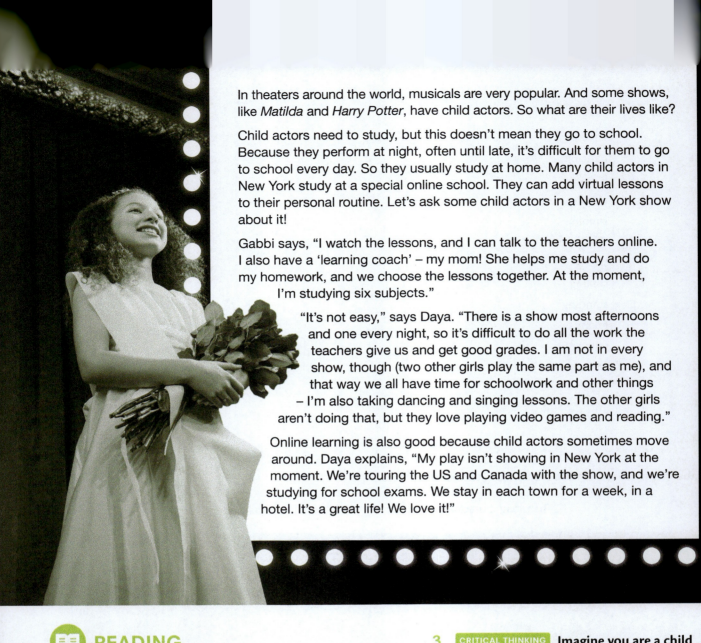

In theaters around the world, musicals are very popular. And some shows, like *Matilda* and *Harry Potter*, have child actors. So what are their lives like?

Child actors need to study, but this doesn't mean they go to school. Because they perform at night, often until late, it's difficult for them to go to school every day. So they usually study at home. Many child actors in New York study at a special online school. They can add virtual lessons to their personal routine. Let's ask some child actors in a New York show about it!

Gabbi says, "I watch the lessons, and I can talk to the teachers online. I also have a 'learning coach' – my mom! She helps me study and do my homework, and we choose the lessons together. At the moment, I'm studying six subjects."

"It's not easy," says Daya. "There is a show most afternoons and one every night, so it's difficult to do all the work the teachers give us and get good grades. I am not in every show, though (two other girls play the same part as me), and that way we all have time for schoolwork and other things – I'm also taking dancing and singing lessons. The other girls aren't doing that, but they love playing video games and reading."

Online learning is also good because child actors sometimes move around. Daya explains, "My play isn't showing in New York at the moment. We're touring the US and Canada with the show, and we're studying for school exams. We stay in each town for a week, in a hotel. It's a great life! We love it!"

READING

1 Read the article about child actors. Do they work all the time? What else do they do?

2 Read the article again and mark the sentences T (true) or F (false). Correct the false statements.

0 Musicals aren't popular around the world.   F
   They are very popular.

1 Child actors all have to continue their education. ☐
_____

2 Theater shows never finish late. ☐
_____

3 All New York child actors study online. ☐
_____

4 They talk to the teachers by phone. ☐
_____

5 When you're in a play, there are often two shows a day. ☐
_____

6 Three different children sometimes play the same part. ☐
_____

7 Daya is performing in New York now. ☐
_____

3 CRITICAL THINKING **Imagine you are a child actor in the theater. What do you like about it? What don't you like about it? Why? Use ideas from this list or your own ideas. Write sentences.**

- getting up early / going to bed late
- organizing your day
- schoolwork and homework
- having fun with friends

_____
_____
_____
_____
_____
_____
_____
_____
_____
_____

DEVELOPING *Writing*

Describing a scene

1 **INPUT** **Read Dalia's email. Why is everyone busy?**

Elias
Dalia@thinkmail.com

Hi Elias,

It's Sunday morning. The sun is shining. I'm sitting in my room. I love sitting here. It's usually quiet, and I like watching the birds in my backyard. But the yard is busy today. My parents are having a big party to celebrate being married for 25 years!!

There's a big tent in the yard. We're having lunch in the tent. My parents are moving tables and chairs. They're laughing and making a lot of noise. There are some people walking into the kitchen. They are carrying big boxes of food and drinks for the party. Uh oh! Now my dad's calling me. He's choosing the party music. His favorite songs are really old, so he wants me to help him!

What are you doing today?

Dalia

2 **ANALYZE** **Match the parts of the phrases. Then read the email again and check your answers.**

0	watching	a	big boxes
1	choosing	b	the birds
2	having	c	party music
3	moving	d	tables and chairs
4	carrying	e	a party

3 **PLAN** **Imagine it's Sunday morning. Use the ideas below and make notes.**

a Choose a place:
- the shopping center
- your house
- the beach
- another place

b What are you doing? What's happening near you? Who can you see and what are they doing? Use these verbs to help you.

buy | have | listen | play | read | sit | watch

_____
_____
_____
_____
_____
_____

c Something happens – it changes things. What happens?

_____
_____
_____
_____
_____
_____

4 **PRODUCE** **Use your notes to write an email to a friend about your Sunday morning. Use the email in Exercise 1 to help you. Write about 60 words.**

✏ WRITING TIP: Starting an email

Start with *Hi* + your friend's name and a comma (,).
Then start the email on the next line.

1 🔊 8.02 **Listen to a boy calling his sister and choose the correct answer.**

1 Right now, he is in the hotel *bedroom / lobby*.

2 After the call, he is going to *Buckingham Palace / the theater*.

2 🔊 8.02 **Listen again and complete the sentences with one word.**

0 Ricky's sister's name is ____*Petra*____ .

1 Ricky is on a class trip to _____ .

2 From his hotel room, he can see some girls riding _____ .

3 He can see a couple wearing formal _____ .

4 His sister thinks the couple is going to the _____ .

5 She forgets that Ricky is going see *The Lion King* _____ .

6 Ricky is wearing nice _____ and his best blue _____ .

7 Petra wants Ricky to call her again _____ .

DIALOGUE

3 🔊 8.03 **Listen to Stefan interviewing Alicia for a school project. How many questions does he ask her?**

_____

4 🔊 8.03 **Listen again and complete the conversation.**

Stefan Hi, Alicia! I'd like to ask you some questions. Is that OK?

Alicia Yeah, sure. What about?

Stefan What do you like doing in the evenings?

Alicia You mean, after school? Well, I like
0 *chatting with friends online* , and I love
1 _____ .

Stefan And what about the weekends?

Alicia On Saturdays, I help clean the house. I like 2 _____ , but I hate 3 _____ the dishes. And on Sundays, I like 4 _____ with my friends at the park or 5 _____ to the movies.

Stefan Thanks, Alicia. Now I can finish my school project.

Alicia Good thing! It's only ten minutes until class!

5 **Now Stefan is interviewing his grandpa. Put Grandpa's answers in the correct order.**

Stefan Grandpa, can I ask you some questions, please?

Grandpa Yes, of course. What do you want to know?

Stefan Well, what do you like doing in the evenings?

Grandpa 0 movies / I / watching / love / .
I love watching movies.

Stefan And what about the weekends?

Grandpa 1 On / I / at / the / soccer club / Saturdays, / like / friends / meeting / my / .

_____

2 I / On / visit / usually / house / Sundays, / your / .

_____

3 family / seeing / I / my / love / .

_____

4 I / don't / your music / listening / like / to / But / always / .

_____

Stefan Thanks a lot, Grandpa.

6 **Imagine that Stefan is interviewing you. Complete the answers to his questions so they are true for you.**

Stefan What do you like doing in the evenings?

You I like _____ , and I love _____ .

Stefan What about the weekend?

You On Saturdays, I like _____ , and on Sundays, I like _____ .

Stefan What do you hate doing?

You I hate _____ .

Stefan And what are you doing now?

You I'm _____ .

Train to TH!NK

Memorizing

7 🔊 8.02 **Listen to Ricky and Petra again. Read the questions (1–5) that Petra asks Ricky. Can you remember Ricky's answers to the questions? Write them down.**

1 How's your class trip going?

_____!

2 What's your room like?

_____!

3 What are you doing now?

_____.

4 What are you doing tonight?
Petra, _____ , remember?

5 Are you wearing a suit, ha ha?
What _____ ?
_____!

8 🔊 8.02 **Listen one more time and check your answers.**

TOWARDS A2 Key for Schools

EXAM SKILLS: READING
Answering multiple-choice questions

1 Read Monika's email to her friend Paulo and answer the questions.

1 Where is Monika? _____
2 What does she want to see there? _____

> **Paulo**
> Monika@thinkmail.com
>
> Hi Paulo,
>
> How are you? I'm on holiday – well, you know that, right? –
> and I'm having a great time here in Granada. We're staying in a nice
> hotel near the city centre. It's small, but it's cheap and very comfortable, and we like it.
> The people who work here speak good English. That's great, because my family doesn't speak
> Spanish! Well, I know a few words now – *gracias* and *por favor*, that kind of thing! I can say
> *Tengo hambre*, too. That means 'I'm hungry', and you know me, I'm always hungry!
>
> Granada is a cool place. The famous Alhambra palace is here. It's very beautiful. And it's a
> great place for Flamenco, too. I love Flamenco dancing and I want to see some here. Oh, just
> a minute – my mum says that Dad is on his tablet and he's getting tickets for a Flamenco show
> tonight here in the city! Great!
>
> Hope you're well. Please write soon, OK?
>
> Monika

2 Read the email again. Choose the correct answers (A, B or C).

0 Monika's family are staying in a _____ hotel.
　A big　　　　　　　Ⓑ comfortable　　　C expensive

1 The people at the hotel _____ English.
　A like　　　　　　　B don't understand　C understand

2 Monika knows _____ words in Spanish.
　A some　　　　　　B a lot of　　　　　C no

3 In Granada there is a famous _____ .
　A palace　　　　　B dance clubs　　　C cool place

4 Monika's _____ has a tablet.
　A father　　　　　B mother　　　　　C Flamenco

5 Monika's father _____ a Flamenco show.
　A isn't getting tickets for　B is buying tickets for　C is reading a book about

📖 READING TIP

When the questions about a text are multiple choice, it means you have to choose the one correct answer
from three or four possibilities.

- Look for items that are grammatically wrong. For example, in the following question, A is wrong because
  we can't have 'a' before a vowel, and C is wrong because we can't use 'some' before a singular noun.

  He's eating _____ apple.

  A a　**B** an　**C** some

- Look for words that have similar meanings. For example, in Question 5 of Exercise 2, 'buying' and 'getting'
  have the same meaning.

- You must check all three (or four) options before you decide which one is correct.

CONSOLIDATION

🎧 LISTENING

1 🔊 8.04 **Listen to Daniela and circle the correct answers (A, B, or C).**

1 Daniela's birthday is …
  A October 20th.
  B October 21st.
  C October 1st.

2 Daniela's camera is a present from …
  A her grandparents.
  B her brother.
  C her mother and father.

3 Daniela's favorite season is …
  A winter.
  B fall.
  C summer.

2 🔊 8.04 **Listen again and complete the words.**

1 Daniela is f_____ .
2 She thinks Ipswich isn't e_____ .
3 Daniela is taking d_____ lessons.
4 Daniela has special s_____ for dancing.
5 Daniela's friends like s_____ .
6 Daniela likes w_____ on cold days.

🔍 GRAMMAR

3 **Circle the correct options.**

Bella Hi, Kurt. What ¹*are / is* you doing?

Kurt Oh, hi, Bella. ²*I wait / I'm waiting* for my dad. And you?

Bella I'm doing some shopping. I'm not ³*buying / buy* much – just some stuff for school. Hey, you have new headphones. They look great!

Kurt Yeah, thanks! ⁴*I'm listening / I listen* to a lot of music. Waiting is boring! I ⁵*can't / don't can* wait without music!

Bella What ⁶*do you listen / are you listening* to right now?

Kurt It's some violin music. I really like ⁷*listen / listening* to violin music.

Bella ⁸*Can you / Do you can* play the violin, Kurt?

Kurt No, I ⁹*can't / can*. But I often ¹⁰*listen / am listening* to it!

4 **Charlie is showing Eva a video on his phone. Put the words in order to make sentences.**

0 is / Liam / brother / This / my / .
  This is my brother Liam.

1 an old people's home / He's / arriving at / .
  _____

2 meeting / He / his friends / is / .
  _____

3 Liam's / today / the guitar / his friends / playing /with / .
  _____

4 are / at the old people's home / They / giving / a concert / .
  _____

5 a chair / is / on / Liam / sitting / .
  _____

6 next to / is / him / My friend Amanda / standing / .
  _____

7 Beatles / singing / songs / They're / old / .
  _____

8 are / The / with / them / old people / singing / .
  _____

🔤 VOCABULARY

5 **Put the words from the list into three groups. Give each group a title. Then write one more word in each group.**

> August | dress | February | golf | gymnastics | jeans
> sweater | June | May | sneakers | surfing | tennis

1 months	2	3

6 **Complete the sentences with the words from the list. There are two extra words.**

> cheer | dance | dancing | second
> summer | talk | two | watching

1 My birthday is the _____ of March.
2 I have a problem with my foot, so I can't _____ tonight.
3 Every week, I _____ to my grandparents in Mexico on the phone.
4 I like listening to music, but I don't like _____ to it!
5 We always _____ when our team wins.
6 It's great here in the _____ when the weather is hot.

DIALOGUE

7 🔊 **8.05** **Put the conversations in order. Then listen and check.**

Conversation 1

☐ **Erin** Great idea! I love baking. Let's check that we have everything we need.

☐ **Erin** No, it's five o'clock. The stores close at five thirty.

☐ **Erin** I'm really bored.

☐ **Dana** Me, too. Why don't we go into town? We can go shopping.

☐ **Dana** Oh yes! OK, how about making a cake?

Conversation 2

☐ **Rico** OK, it's no big deal. We can stay here in my house. I have a good book to read.

☐ **Rico** Hey, how about going for a walk?

☐ **Rico** Yes, I'm sure I can find one for you.

☐ **Sara** Great idea! I love reading. Do you have a book for me, too?

☐ **Sara** No thanks! It's cold outside. And I don't like walking very much.

📖 READING

8 **Read the phone conversation. Then complete the sentences with the correct information.**

Noah Hey, Ella, what are you doing?

Ella I'm talking to you on the phone, ha ha!

Noah Yes, very funny. But seriously – what are you doing?

Ella Nothing really. I'm just sitting in my room. Why?

Noah How about coming to the park? That's where I am now!

Ella The park? Why? What's happening in the park?

Noah There's a race today. It's a ten-kilometer run. My parents are running in it.

Ella Are they crazy? It's winter! It's cold, and it's raining.

Noah It isn't raining very much. And I'm wearing a warm coat and shoes. So, I'm OK.

Ella Well, no thanks. I like being warm, not cold.

Noah OK, it's no big deal. Oh, and Mark Watson's running in the race. I can see him, too.

Ella Really? Mark Watson from our school?

Noah Yes, him. And at the moment, he's first – he's winning!

Ella Right, I'm putting my coat on, and I'm leaving the house now.

Noah Really?

Ella Yes – Mark Watson's there, so I want to be there, too!

Noah Oh, OK. See you soon then!

1 Ella is in _____ .

2 Noah is in _____ .

3 There's a _____-kilometer race today.

4 Noah's _____ and _____ are running in the race.

5 Noah _____ cold because he's _____ a warm coat.

6 Ella doesn't like _____ .

7 Mark Watson is a boy from their _____ .

8 Mark is _____ the race.

9 Ella is _____ the house because she wants to _____ .

✏️ WRITING

9 **Write a short dialogue between two friends. Write about 60 words. Use these ideas to help you.**

- one friend is bored
- the other friend suggests something to do
- the first friend doesn't like the idea very much
- the second friend suggests another thing to do (go for a walk, go to the movies, play video games, etc.)

9 WHO'S HUNGRY?

Grammar rap!

GRAMMAR

must / mustn't → SB p.86

1 ⭐☆☆ **Complete the sentences with *must* or *mustn't*.**

My very healthy mom says:

0 I ___mustn't___ drink too much soda.
1 I _____ eat more vegetables.
2 I _____ eat snacks or chocolate before meals.
3 I _____ go to bed late.
4 I _____ play sports after school.
5 I _____ drink more water.

2 ⭐☆☆ **Circle the correct options.**

0 **A** Dad, do we have any fruit?
   B No, we don't. I (must) / mustn't buy some.
1 **A** Do you want to come to my house after school?
   B I can't. I've got a clarinet lesson tomorrow so I *must / mustn't* practice tonight.
2 **A** What day is it today?
   B It's Wednesday. We have PE this morning. You *must / mustn't* forget your PE clothes.
3 **A** What a cute hamster! Can we take it home?
   B OK, but you *must / mustn't* take care of it.
4 **A** I'm not ready yet.
   B Hurry up then. We *must / mustn't* miss the bus.
5 **A** I'm ready, Mom.
   B Good. The movie starts in an hour, and we *must / mustn't* be late.
6 **A** Hey Dad, can I have one of these apples?
   B Yes, but you *must / mustn't* wash it before you eat it.

3 ⭐⭐⭐ **Complete the sentences with *must* (✓) or *mustn't* (✗) and a verb from the list.**

be | buy | eat | finish | forget
give | remember | wash | write

0 Ellie _____must write_____ an email to her friend Maria in Colombia. (✓)
1 Marcus _____ home late today. (✗)
2 Helena _____ to take her tablet to school. (✓)
3 Oscar and Joao _____ to clean their bedrooms. (✗)
4 Dario _____ the book back to Jose. (✓)
5 Frida and Sofia _____ a present for their friend Jana. (✓)
6 Mateo _____ his homework before dinner. (✓)
7 We _____ any food in the classroom. (✗)
8 We _____ our hands before we eat lunch. (✓)

4 ⭐⭐⭐ **Write five things you *must* or *mustn't* do this year.**

0 *I must learn a lot of new English words.*
1 _____
2 _____
3 _____
4 _____
5 _____

can (asking for permission) → SB p.87

5 ⭐⭐☆ **Put the words in order to make questions.**

0 we / Can / the hockey game / Saturday / on / go / to / ?
   Can we go to the hockey game on Saturday?
1 have / I / Can / fries / dinner / for / ?
   _____
2 I / Can / invite / Toby / to / my birthday party / ?
   _____
3 go / we / Can / the park / to / school / after / ?
   _____
4 call / I / Can / my sister / ?
   _____
5 I / wear / Can / green / sweater / your / today / ?
   _____

82

6 ★★☆ **Match the children's questions with Dad's answers.**

0 Can I take your laptop to school with me?

1 Can we go swimming on Sunday?

2 Can I go to Kate's house after school tonight?

3 Can Mike and I go climbing this weekend?

a No, we can't. The pool is closed this weekend.

b Yes, of course you can. But don't come home late.

c Well, OK. But be careful.

d No, you can't. I need it for work.

I'd like ... / Would you like ...?   → SB p.89

7 ★☆☆ **Write sentences using 'd like / Would ... like.**

0 I / tomato soup
I'd like tomato soup.

1 my mom / steak salad
_____

2 what / you / for dessert / ?
_____

3 Dad / ice cream for dessert / ?
_____

8 ★★☆ **Put the conversation in order.**

☐ **Waiter** (five minutes later) Are you ready to order?

☐ **Waiter** Four soups, OK. And what would you like for the main course?

☐ **Waiter** And finally, any drinks?

☐ **Waiter** OK, so would you like a starter?

[1] **Waiter** Good evening. Would you like a table for four?

☐ **Customer** Yes, please.

☐ **Customer** Yes, we are.

☐ **Customer** Just water for everyone, thanks.

☐ **Customer** We'd like one cheese salad, one steak with potatoes and vegetables, one pizza, and one burger and fries, please.

☐ **Customer** Yes, please. We'd like two tomato soups and two vegetable soups.

PRONUNCIATION
Intonation – giving two choices
Go to page 121. 🎧

9 ★★☆ **Look at the menu on page 88 of the Student's Book and complete the conversation so it is true for you.**

Waiter Are you ready to order?

You Yes, I am.

Waiter Would you like a starter?

You _____

Waiter And what would you like for the main course?

You _____

Waiter And would you like a dessert?

You _____

Waiter Any drinks?

You Yes, _____

GET IT RIGHT!

like and would like

We use like to say that something is nice.

✓ I like ice cream. It's delicious!

We use would like to ask for something we want or to ask somebody what they want.

✓ I would like a burger, please.

✗ I like a burger, please.

✓ Would you like a burger?

✗ You like a burger?

Circle the correct options.

0 I like / (would like) to come to your house tomorrow.

1 I like / would like a VR headset for my birthday.

2 I like / would like this house, and I'm happy living here.

3 I like / would like traveling to different countries.

4 I like / would like to go shopping on Monday.

5 I'm thirsty. I like / would like a drink of water.

6 When I have time, I like / would like cooking.

VOCABULARY
Food and drinks

→ SB p.86

1 ★☆☆ Look at the pictures and complete the crossword. What's the mystery sentence?

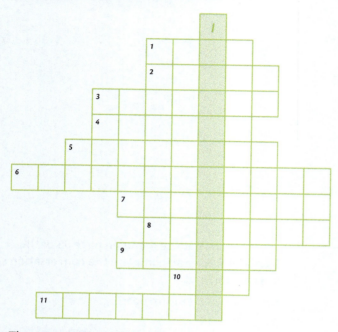

The mystery sentence is: _____

2 ★★☆ Put the letters in order to make food words.

0 We're having _____*beef*_____ with potatoes and vegetables for lunch today. (e b e f)

1 My mom doesn't like _____. (b l a m)

2 I often drink _____ with my breakfast. (l i m k)

3 I sometimes have an _____ after dinner. (p l p a e)

4 I'd like _____ and ice cream for dessert. (s t a r w b i r r e e s)

5 I like most vegetables, but I don't like _____. (a c o r r t s)

Meals

→ SB p.89

3 ★☆☆ Find and circle nine breakfast items in the word snake.

abreadonbutterilkhoneymotoastljamogeggnyogurtatcerealettfruitth

4 ★★☆ Put the words in order to make sentences or questions.

0 you / do / usually / eat / for / breakfast, / What / Dora / ?
What do you usually eat for breakfast, Dora?

1 always / I / eat / an / egg / breakfast / for / .
_____

2 usually / I / eat / toast / .
_____

3 you / lunch / usually / have / for / What / do / ?
_____

4 often / I / have / baked potato / a / .
_____

5 sometimes / have / I / steak / vegetables / with / .
_____

6 do / you / What / usually / drink / meals, / with / your / Dora / ?
_____

7 drink / I / usually / or water / fruit juice / .
_____

5 ★★☆ Check (✓) the things Dora has for breakfast and lunch in Exercise 4.

☐ fruit ☐ pizza ☐ yogurt
☐ toast ☐ spaghetti ☐ cereal
☐ an egg ☐ vegetables ☐ steak
☐ water ☐ baked potato ☐ chicken
☐ coffee ☐ fruit juice ☐ fries

6 ★★★ Write sentences about Luca and Jamie using the words in parentheses.

	always	often	sometimes	never
breakfast	an egg	toast	cereal	yogurt
lunch	coffee	a sandwich	pizza	soup
dinner	soup	pasta	fish	salad

0 *They sometimes have cereal for breakfast.* (sometimes)

1 _____ (always)

2 _____ (often)

3 _____ (never)

4 _____ (sometimes)

5 _____ (often)

📄 REFERENCE

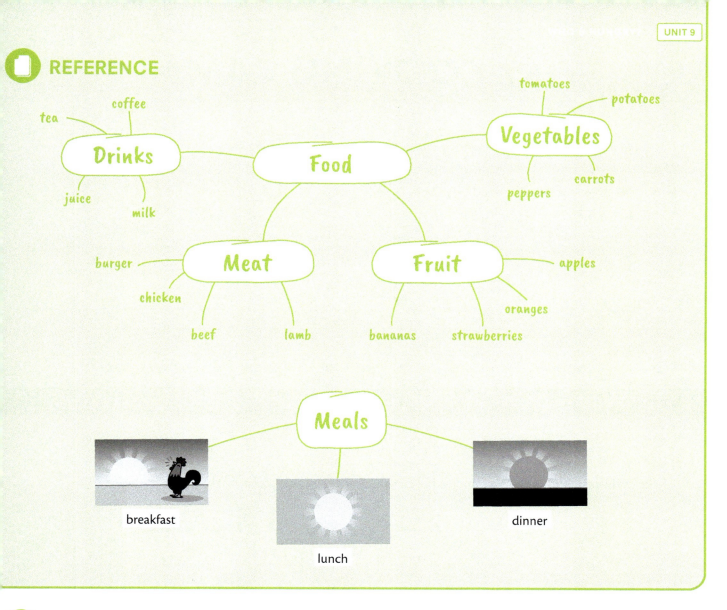

Drinks — tea, coffee, juice, milk

Food

Vegetables — tomatoes, potatoes, carrots, peppers

Meat — burger, chicken, beef, lamb

Fruit — apples, oranges, strawberries, bananas

Meals

breakfast

lunch

dinner

🔤 VOCABULARY *EXTRA*

1 Write the name of each food under the photos. Use words from the photos.

cheese | garlic | grapes | lemon | melon | onion | sour cream

1 _____

2 _____

3 _____

4 _____

5 _____

6 _____

7 _____

2 Put the food from Exercise 1 into the correct category in the table.

dairy	fruit	vegetables
milk	apple	carrot

Mid-term HOLIDAY COOKING CAMP

October 28th, 29th, & 30th

This is the third year of our cooking camp. It's a great way to start cooking for yourself!

Time: mornings from 10 a.m. to 1 p.m., for three days

Open to: boys and girls ages 11–14 years

Price: $45 (includes ingredients)

You can learn to make:

CAKES   PIZZA   HEALTHY SOUPS   FRUIT SMOOTHIES

BREAD   PASTA

★ You must be 11–14 years old.
★ You must love food.
★ You must wear a chef's hat (don't worry, we give you one!).
★ You mustn't be late. There's a lot to learn.
★ And remember! Cooking is fun!

Your teacher Marianne is an excellent cook, and she loves good food. She has family from Spain, Turkey, Italy, and Russia. Marianne loves and cooks food from all of those countries. Come and learn to cook with her.

Our cooking camps are very popular, so sign up now!! Call 212-231-6564 to reserve your place.

READING

1 Read the leaflet for Cooking camp. What can you learn to make? Check (✓) the correct photos.

 A

 B

 C

 D

 E

2 Read the leaflet again and correct the sentences.

0 Cooking camp is in November.
Cooking camp is in October.

1 Cooking camp is for three afternoons.
_____

2 You don't make any drinks.
_____

3 Marianne has family from Germany.
_____

4 You must be 8–11 years old.
_____

5 You mustn't wear any special clothes.
_____

6 You mustn't be on time.
_____

7 Remember that cooking is important.
_____

3 CRITICAL THINKING Answer the questions about the food camp.

1 What things on the list are healthy things to cook?
2 Can you think of one reason why cooking is fun?
3 Think of two reasons why it is important for young people to learn to cook.

4 Complete the questionnaire for the Cooking camp so it is true for you.

COOKING CAMP
Questionnaire

1 What's your name? _____
2 How old are you? _____
3 What is your favorite dish? _____
4 Do you help your parents in the kitchen? _____
5 Can you cook? _____
6 What can you cook? _____

DEVELOPING *Writing*

My birthday meal plan

1 **INPUT** **Read the text about Sam's birthday dinner. What does he never drink on his birthday?**

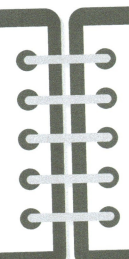

My family usually eats healthy food, like rice and meat with vegetables and fruit for dessert. But on my birthday, we always have a special dinner together. We sometimes have my mom's amazing pizza, and sometimes chicken with hot sauce, fries, and salad (my favorite!). For dessert, we have my favorite ice cream – strawberry. My mom always makes my birthday cake. It's usually chocolate cake. I never drink soda on my birthday. I like lemonade.

2 **ANALYZE** **Answer the questions.**

0 How often does Sam's family eat healthy food?
They usually eat healthy food.

1 What is his favorite birthday meal?
_____

2 What does he have for dessert on his birthday?
_____

3 What does his mother always make him?
_____

4 What does he usually drink on his birthday?
_____

3 **PLAN** **Think about a dinner your family often eats on normal days. Now plan a special birthday meal with your favorite foods. Write your food choices in the table. Use words from the list and your own ideas.**

baked potato | bread | burger | chicken
chocolate | chocolate cake | eggs | fish
fries | fruit | fruit juice | ice cream
meat | milk | pasta | pizza | rice | salad
soda | soup | toast | vegetables | water

	normal meal	special birthday meal
food and drink		

4 **PRODUCE** **Use your notes from Exercise 3 to write a birthday meal plan. Use the text in Exercise 1 to help you. Write about 60 words.**

_____
_____
_____
_____
_____
_____
_____
_____
_____
_____
_____
_____
_____
_____
_____
_____

WRITING TIP: Adding detail

Add more detail to your writing by using adverbs of frequency:

• How often do you eat things?

You can answer this question with *always*, *usually*, *sometimes*, and *never*.

I sometimes have my mom's pizza.
I never drink soda.
I usually have fruit for dessert.
I always have a special birthday lunch with my family.

LISTENING

1 🔊 9.02 **Listen and check (✓) the things on the menu that the family decides to order.**

The BURGER and SALAD BAR
MENU
— STARTERS —
Soup of the day* ☐

Salad bar ☐

— MAIN COURSE —
Our delicious **burgers**!
★ Beef ☐   ★ Lamb ☐   ★ Vegetable ☐

Options from the grill!
★ Chicken ☐   ★ Steak ☐   ★ Fish ☐

— SIDES —
Fries ☐

Baked potato ☐

Vegetables of the day* ☐

Onion rings ☐

— DRINKS —
Lemonade ☐

Soda ☐

Apple juice ☐

Orange juice ☐

Hot tea ☐

Coffee ☐

Water ☐

— DESSERT —
Chef's dessert of the day* ☐

Carrot cake ☐

Ice cream:
★ Strawberry ☐   ★ Chocolate ☐   ★ Vanilla ☐

Look at the board on the wall!

2 🔊 9.02 **Listen again and mark the sentences T (true) or F (false).**

0 You choose your own food at the salad bar. `T`

1 The soup of the day is tomato. ☐

2 Jason loves broccoli and carrots. ☐

3 Jason orders three things. ☐

4 Dad doesn't want a starter. ☐

5 Ashley has a small dessert. ☐

DIALOGUE

3 **Circle the correct options.**

Waiter	Are you ready to ⁰*sit down* / *order*?
Customer 1	Yes, we are.
Waiter	Would you like a ¹*starter* / *main course*?
Customer 1	Yes, please. I'd like tomato soup.
Customer 2	And I'd like vegetable soup.
Waiter	And what would you like for the ²*dessert* / *main course*?
Customer 1	I'd like chicken salad, please.
Customer 2	And I'd like fish and a baked potato, please.
Waiter	And for ³*starter* / *dessert*?
Customer 1	We'd like the chocolate cake, please.
Waiter	Any ⁴*drinks* / *desserts*?
Customer 1	Yes, please. I'd like apple juice.
Customer 2	And I'd like water.

PHRASES FOR FLUENCY → SB p.90

4 **Complete the conversations with phrases from the list.**

Of course. | Be careful! | a little | the thing is

Conversation 1
A Can you take these plates to the table?
B OK.
A _____ Don't drop them.
B It's OK, Dad. Don't worry!

Conversation 2
A What's for dinner?
B It's pizza.
A Oh, no.
B What's wrong with pizza? I love it.
A Well, _____ , I don't like tomatoes.

Conversation 3
A Is there any cheese on the baked potato?
B Yes, there is, and there's _____ butter, too.

Conversation 4
A Would you like some vegetables with your steak?
B _____ I love vegetables.

SUM IT UP

1 **Put the letters in order to find the food words.**

What's on Mario's pizza?

0 s e e c h e   _cheese_

1 r e p s p e p   _____

2 k i c e n c h   _____

3 o e s t o m t a   _____

What would Evalina like for dinner?

4 k e a s t   _____

5 t o p o e s t a   _____

6 d a s a l   _____

What's in Emma's dessert?

7 c o c h l a t e o   _____

8 c i e r e c a m   _____

9 r a w s t e r r i e b s   _____

10 n a b a n a   _____

C A F É _____

starters

_____

_____

drinks

_____

_____

main courses

_____

_____

_____

_____

desserts

_____

_____

_____

2 **Complete the menu. Use food and drink words from the unit.**

- Think of a name for your café.
- Create a milkshake or a smoothie.
- Make a special pizza for your café.
- Create meals with the food words.
- Create one unusual meal.

For example: *Strawberry and Orange Salad* or *Carrot and Orange Soup*

3 **Imagine you have a customer at your café. Complete the conversation.**

Waiter   Hello and welcome to Café [1]_____ .

Customer 1   Hello. We'd like a table for two.

Waiter   OK. Follow me, please.

(5 minutes later)

Waiter   Are you ready to order now?

Customer 1   Yes, we are.

Waiter   Would you like a starter?

Customer 1   Yes, please. [2]_____ and my friend [3]_____ .

Waiter   And what [4]_____ for the main course?

Customer 1   [5]_____ , please.

Customer 2   And [6]_____ .

Waiter   And for dessert?

Customer 1   [7]_____ , please.

Customer 2   And [8]_____ .

Waiter   Any drinks?

Customer 1   Yes, please. [9]_____ , and my friend [10]_____ .

Grammar rap!
▶29

GRAMMAR

Simple past: *was / wasn't; were / weren't; there was / were* → SB p.94

1 ★☆☆ **Circle the correct options.**

0 You *was* / *were* late.

1 It *wasn't* / *weren't* his book.

2 I *was* / *were* at home yesterday.

3 We *was* / *were* at the movies.

4 They *wasn't* / *weren't* at the hockey game last night.

5 She *was* / *were* my best friend.

2 ★★☆ **Complete the sentences with** *was, were, wasn't,* **or** *weren't.*

0 I _____was_____ (✓) born in Mexico City.

1 My grandma _____ (✗) a pilot.

2 Adam and Jay _____ (✓) in the park yesterday.

3 We _____ (✗) at my aunt's house last night.

4 Leon _____ (✗) at the basketball court on Sunday.

5 It _____ (✓) my birthday yesterday.

3 ★★★ **Complete the text with the correct simple past form of** *to be.*

The Montgolfier brothers ^{0}_____were_____ the inventors of the hot-air balloon. They ^{1}_____ (✓) French. Their names ^{2}_____ (✓) Joseph-Michel and Jacques-Étienne. Joseph-Michel ^{3}_____ (✓) born in 1740, and Jacques-Étienne ^{4}_____ (✓) born in 1745. There ^{5}_____ (✓) sixteen children in the family. Their father ^{6}_____ (✗) an inventor. He ^{7}_____ (✓) a paper manufacturer. The first balloon flight ^{8}_____ (✓) in June of 1783. There ^{9}_____ (✗) any passengers. There ^{10}_____ (✓) no one on the balloon. The second flight ^{11}_____ (✓) in Paris in September of 1783. This time, there ^{12}_____ (✓) three passengers, but the passengers ^{13}_____ (✗) people. They ^{14}_____ (✓) a chicken, a duck, and a sheep.

Simple past: *Was he ...? / Were you ...?* → SB p.95

4 ★☆☆ **Match the questions with the answers.**

0 Were you born in Rome?
1 Was your grandfather a chef?
2 Was Valentina an astronaut?
3 Was it your phone?
4 Was I late to the party?
5 Were you and I on time?
6 Were Sandra and Joel at the youth club yesterday?

a No, he wasn't.
b Yes, you were!
c Yes, it was.
d No, we weren't.
e Yes, I was.
f No, they weren't.
g Yes, she was.

5 ★★★ **Put the words in order to make questions. Then look at the text in Exercise 3 and answer the questions.**

0 Were / the / inventors / brothers / Montgolfier / ?
Were the Montgolfier brothers inventors?
Yes, they were.

1 they / Italian / Were / ?
_____

2 Was / Joseph-Michel / in 1740 / born / ?
_____
_____

3 Was / inventor / an / their / father / ?
_____
_____

4 the / Was / in / flight / first / June of 1795 / ?
_____
_____

5 flight / second / Prague / in / Was / the / ?
_____
_____

6 Were / there / passengers / any / ?
_____
_____

Simple past: regular verbs → SB p.97

6 ★☆☆ **Complete the table with the correct simple past of the verbs in the list.**

believe | carry | cry | finish
help | like | live | study | work

+ -ed	+ -d	+ -ied
finished		

7 ★★☆ **Put the words in order to make sentences. Put the verbs in the simple past.**

0 uncle / My / study / college / in / medicine / .
My uncle studied medicine in college.

1 finish / degree / his / He / 2010 / in / .
_____

2 at / hospital / a / He / work / Denver / in / .
_____

3 in / He / San Francisco / three / years / for / live / .
_____

4 like / He / California / very / much / .
_____

5 move / He / Los Angeles / to / 2014 / in / .
_____

8 ★★☆ **Complete the text with the simple past form of the verbs in parentheses.**

DAVID ATTENBOROUGH

The famous scientist David Attenborough
0 _____*lived*_____ (live) in London as a child.
He **1**_____ (study) at Cambridge University
and later in London. In 1950, Attenborough
2_____ (marry) Jane Oriel, and they had two
children. He **3**_____ (work) for the BBC for
many years as a producer, but he **4**_____
(want) to make shows about nature. In 1972,
he **5**_____ (stop) working at the BBC and
6_____ (start) to make nature shows. He
soon **7**_____ (return) to the BBC and made
many famous series, including *Life on Earth*
in 1976, with 96 episodes! Over many years,
Attenborough and his teams **8**_____
(discover) new ways to film animals and plants.
He **9**_____ (travel) to all seven continents,
and millions of people **10**_____ (watch) his
programs.

9 ★★★ **Complete the text with the simple past form of the verbs in parentheses.**

Florence Nightingale

Florence Nightingale **0**_____*was*_____ (be) a famous
English nurse. She **1**_____ (be) born
in Florence, Italy, in 1820. Later, her parents
2_____ (move) back to England. As a
child, she **3**_____ (like) helping others.
She **4**_____ (care) for sick people and
animals. She **5**_____ (want) to be a nurse.
In 1851, she **6**_____ (work) as a nurse in
Germany. In 1853, there **7**_____ (be) a war.
It **8**_____ (be) called the Crimean War.
They **9**_____ (need) nurses,
so Florence **10**_____
(sail) with nurses to help.
They **11**_____ (help) the
British soldiers there. Life
12_____ (not be) easy.
The war **13**_____ (end)
in 1856. Florence Nightingale
14_____ (return) to
England as a hero. She
15_____ (die) in
London in 1910.

PRONUNCIATION
Simple past regular verbs Go to page 121. 🎧

GET IT RIGHT!

was / wasn't and *were / weren't*
**We use *was*, *wasn't*, *were*, and *weren't* to talk
about the past. We use *am*, *am not*, *is*, *isn't*, *are*, and
aren't to talk about now.**
✓ *Yesterday was my birthday.*
✗ *Yesterday is my birthday.*
Correct the sentences.

0 Geoff isn't at school yesterday.
Geoff wasn't at school yesterday.

1 There is a great movie on TV last night.
_____

2 Hello! I was very happy to see you.
_____

3 All my friends are there for my birthday last night.
_____

4 Is Laura with you yesterday evening?
_____

5 Gigi was worried about her exam today.
_____

6 They aren't late for school yesterday.
_____

VOCABULARY

Time expressions: past

→ SB p.94

1 ★☆☆ **Complete the table with the words from the list.**

> afternoon | evening | ~~month~~
> morning | night | Saturday
> 3 o'clock | year | 6 p.m.
> 10:30 | 1969 | 2015

last	in
month	
at	**yesterday**

2 ★☆☆ **Complete the dialogues with _at_, _in_, _last_, and _yesterday_.**

0 A Where were you _____last_____ night?
  B I was at home.

1 A Were you at school _____ afternoon?
  B Yes, I was.

2 A Was Jaime at the party _____ Saturday?
  B No, he was at home.

3 A Was your dad born _____ 1980?
  B No, he wasn't.

4 A Was Tim still at school _____ 5 p.m. this evening?
  B Yes, he was.

3 ★★☆ **Where were you? Write sentences with _at_, _last_, and _yesterday_ and the time if necessary.**

0 (at) _I was on the bus at 8 o'clock._

1 (at) _____

2 (last) _____

3 (yesterday) _____

The weather

→ SB p.97

4 ★★☆ **Complete the sentences and the crossword with the same words.**

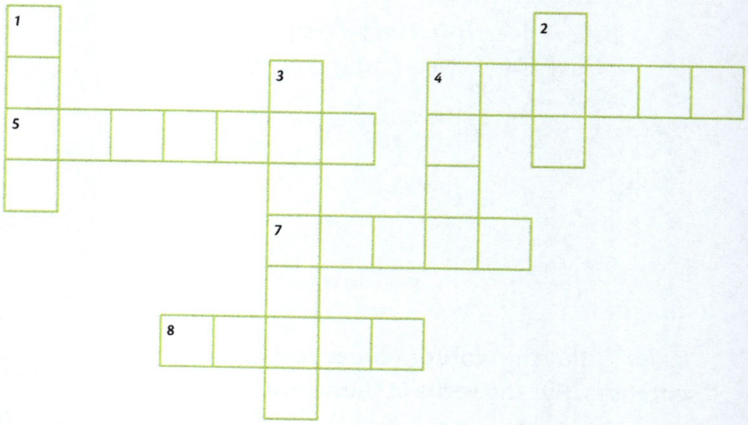

[crossword grid]

ACROSS

4 Today it's _____ , so we don't need our sunglasses.
5 It's _____ , so don't forget your umbrella.
7 It's _____ , so it's a great day to fly your kite.
8 It's _____ – there are a lot of people on the beach today.

DOWN

1 Today is beautiful and _____ . Let's sit outside.
2 Drink a lot of water today – it's very _____ !
3 You can make a snowman today. It's _____ .
4 It's _____ today, so don't forget to wear warm clothes.

5 ★★☆ **Circle the correct options in these phone conversations.**

1 A What's the weather like?
  B It's ⁰(sunny) / cloudy. I'm wearing sunglasses.
  A Is it ¹cold / hot?
  B Yes, it is. I'm wearing a T-shirt. What's the weather like there?
  A It's very ²cloudy / windy here. Listen. Can you hear it?
  B Yes, I can.

2 A What's the weather like?
  B It's ³raining / cloudy. I can't play soccer outside today.
  A Is it ⁴cold / hot?
  B Yes, it is. I'm wearing a sweater and a coat. What's the weather like there?
  A It's ⁵snowing / windy here. We can't go to school today because we can't get out of the house.
  B Really?

6 ★★★ **Write sentences about the weather today. What can or can't you do?**

_____
_____
_____
_____

REFERENCE

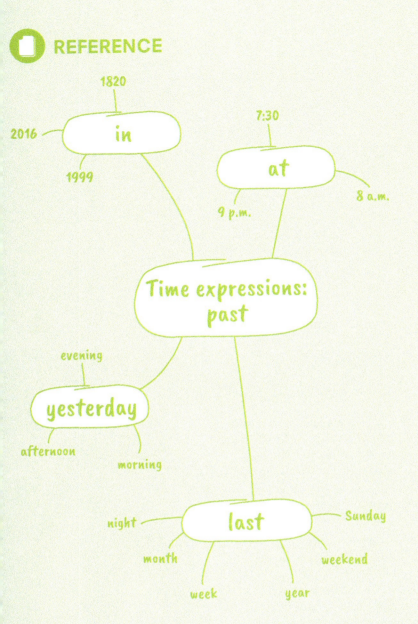

1820
2016
1999

in

7:30

at

9 p.m.
8 a.m.

Time expressions: past

evening

yesterday

afternoon
morning

night

last

Sunday

month
weekend
week
year

The weather

It's sunny.

It's cloudy.

It's hot.

It's raining.

It's snowing.

It's windy.

It's cold.

It's warm.

VOCABULARY *EXTRA*

1 Match the definitions with the words from the list.

after | at noon | at midnight | before | early | late

0 in the middle of the day: ___at noon___
1 before something starts: _____
2 earlier than something else: _____
3 after something starts: _____
4 at 12 o'clock at night: _____
5 in the time following something else: _____

2 Put the letters in order to make words.

0 Please don't be ___late___ for the movie. We mustn't miss the beginning! (a l t e)
1 My little sister's birthday in June is _____ my birthday in May. (t e f a r)
2 Can you come _____ the party starts to help me with the food? (e o e r f b)
3 The music festival starts _____ on Saturday. (t a o n o n)
4 To get a good seat at the concert, you need to arrive very _____ (e y l r a)
5 The last bus home from the city center is _____ (t a d g h i i m n t)

Flying MACHINES

A

Do you like flying? Did you know that there are different ways to explore the skies? Here we look at two incredible flying inventions from France!

On July 25, 1909, the French aviator Louis Blériot flew a monoplane (a plane with one pair of wings) across the English Channel - the sea between France and England. He developed the first monoplane with a pilot, and he was the first person to fly from one country to another across the sea! The plane didn't look very strong, but it only took 36 minutes and 30 seconds to fly the 35 kilometers from France to England. An English newspaper gave him a prize of £1,000. In those days, most people only dreamed of flying, because it wasn't possible for them.

B

The invention of the jet plane in the 1930s changed that. Jet planes can go very fast, very far, and carry hundreds of people. By the 1960s, air travel as we know today became possible. Now people, and not just rich people, fly all over the world.

And inventors are still finding new ways to fly! Another Frenchman, Franky Zapata, was a jet ski World Champion. When he stopped racing, he invented a hoverboard called the Flyboard Air. It uses technology similar to drones, and jet plane fuel. On August 4, 2019, 110 years after Blériot, Zapata crossed the Channel on his Flyboard Air, at a top speed of 170 kilometers an hour, and arrived safely on the south coast of England in 22 minutes. He looked like a superhero in a comic!

Can you imagine people on hoverboards flying everywhere in the future? Who knows! In 1909, no one imagined people flying away on vacation! How quickly things change!

C

READING

1   Read the article about flying machines. Put the photos in order from old to new (1–3).

2   Read the article again. What do these numbers mean?

   0 2019   *Franky Zapata crossed the Channel on the Flyboard Air.*
   1 35   _____
   2 1909   _____
   3 22   _____
   4 1,000   _____
   5 170   _____

3   **CRITICAL THINKING**   Read the article again and check (✓) the words you think describe Zapata's hoverboard. Why did you choose each word? Write your reasons.

- fun   ☐   • climate-friendly ☐
- expensive   ☐   • easy to use   ☐
- dangerous   ☐   • a great idea   ☐

_____
_____
_____
_____

DEVELOPING Writing

A short biography

1 **INPUT** **Read the fact file and biography of Alicia Keys. Where was she born?**

A Personal details

Alicia Keys is an American singer, pianist, and songwriter. Her real name is Alicia Augello-Cook. She was born in New York on January 25, 1981, and lived in a poor area. She is married to a DJ, Swizz Beatz, and they have two sons.

B Professional

Alicia went to the Professional Performing Arts School in New York and studied classical piano. A record company gave her a contract when she was only 15. She has many hit songs and successful albums.

C Charity work

Alicia helped start a charity in Africa called Keep a Child Alive, which helps sick children, and she organizes concerts to raise money every year. She also tries to help fight racism and poverty.

FACT FILE

Alicia Keys

1 Date of birth: January 25, 1981

2 Nationality: American

3 Education: Professional Performing Arts School, New York

4 Real name: Alicia Augello-Cook

5 Family: married to DJ Swizz Beatz, two sons

6 Place of birth: New York

7 Job: singer, musician, songwriter

8 Big break: Record contract in 1996, age 15

9 Charity work: Keep a Child Alive (charity in Africa, helps sick children)

2 **ANALYZE** **Match sections 1–9 in the fact file with paragraphs A–C.**

Paragraph A: Section(s): _____

Paragraph B: Section(s): _____

Paragraph C: Section(s): _____

3 **Read paragraphs A and B again and find three facts that are not in the fact file. Then match them with the correct sections in the fact file.**

4 **PLAN** **Use the information in the list to complete the fact file about Millie Bobby Brown.**

actress, producer | British | ~~Millie Bobby Brown~~
2016, Eleven in *Stranger Things*, age 12
Marbella, Spain (now lives in the US)
Millie Bobby Brown | February 19, 2004
two sisters, one brother
UNICEF ambassador (youngest ever)

FACT FILE

Millie Bobby Brown

1 Nationality:

2 Place of birth:

3 Date of birth:

4 Real name:

5 Family:

6 Job:

7 Big break:

8 Charity work:

WRITING TIP: Organization

A biography includes a lot of information, so it needs good organization.

One way to do this is with paragraphs and headings, like in the text about Alicia Keys:

- A Personal details
- B Professional
- C Charity work

5 **PRODUCE** **Use the fact file to write a short biography of Millie Bobby Brown. You can use the internet to find more information. Write about 70 words.**

🎧 LISTENING

1 Look at the picture and guess the answers to the questions.

1 Who is the man in the photo?

_____

2 What did he write about?

_____

2 🔊 10.02 **Listen to Tom talking about a writer. Circle the correct options.**

0 Tom's hero was a (writer) / artist.

1 His most famous book was *Narnia* / *The Jungle Book*.

2 His parents were *English* / *Indian*.

3 His father was *a doctor* / *an artist*.

4 Rudyard Kipling *loved* / *hated* India.

5 He was *happy* / *unhappy* with the Holloways.

6 He *loved* / *hated* books.

7 He was *happy* / *unhappy* at school in Devon.

8 After school he lived in *Italy* / *India*.

9 He worked for a *newspaper* / *university*.

3 🔊 10.02 **Listen again and complete the text with the correct words.**

Rudyard Kipling's parents were English.
They ⁰___*moved*___ to India. His father was an
artist, and he worked at a school of Art in Bombay
(which is now called Mumbai). Kipling loved
India. He loved the ¹_____ and the culture.
However, he didn't have a happy childhood.
His parents wanted him to go to ²_____
in England. When he was six years old, he lived
with a ³_____ , the Holloways, in a seaside
⁴_____ in England. Mrs. Holloway was very
bad to him. He ⁵_____ life there, and he
was very unhappy. Luckily, he ⁶_____ books.
He loved books. They ⁷_____ him from his
unhappy life.

DIALOGUE

4 Complete the conversation with the past simple of the verbs in parentheses. Then put the conversation in order.

1	Ben	⁰___*Were*___ (be) you at home yesterday?
☐	Ben	Did they? ¹_____ (be) they good?
☐	Ben	²_____ (be) it a good party?
☐	Ben	Oh, I remember. It ³_____ (be) your cousin's birthday yesterday, right?
☐	Sam	Yes, they ⁴_____ (be) very good.
☐	Sam	Yes, it ⁵_____ (be). I loved it.
☐	Sam	Yes, it ⁶_____ (be). Her brothers are in a band. They ⁷_____ (play) at her party.
☐	Sam	No, I ⁸_____ (not be). I ⁹_____ (be) at my cousin's house.

Train to TH!NK

Sequencing

5 Complete the sequence with words from the list.

> And then | Finally | First

> _____ > Then > _____
> After that > _____

6 Order the events in Rudyard Kipling's life. Then complete the sentences with sequencing words from Exercise 5.

Rudyard Kipling (1865–1936)

☐ _____ , he died in London in 1936.

☐ _____ he lived in a seaside town in England with the Holloway family.

☐ _____*First*_____ , Rudyard Kipling lived in India.

☐ _____ he moved to a school in Devon.

☐ _____ , he moved back to India, and he worked for a newspaper.

TOWARDS A2 Key for Schools

EXAM SKILLS: LISTENING
Listening for key words

1 🔊 10.03 **Listen and tick (✓) the months you hear.**

January ☐ | February ☐ | March ☐ | April ☐ | May ☐ | June ☐ | July ☐
August ☐ | September ☐ | October ☐ | November ☐ | December ☐

🎧 **LISTENING TIP**

- First, learn to listen for key words, for example, the months of the year.
- Next, you need to complete the profile. Listen carefully for the dates, the jobs and the places.
Remember! You don't need to understand everything.

2 🔊 10.04 **Listen and circle the correct options to complete Claude Monet's profile.**

Claude Monet

0 Job
~~writer~~ / (painter)
1 Nationality
French / Italian
2 Born
14th September / November 1840
3 Mother's job
singer / actor
4 Father's job
gardener / grocer
5 September 1870
He lived in London / New York.
6 May 1871
He moved to Germany / Holland.
7 May 1883
He moved to Giverny in France / Belgium.
8 Died
5th June / December 1926

3 🔊 10.05 **Listen and complete Vincent Van Gogh's profile.**

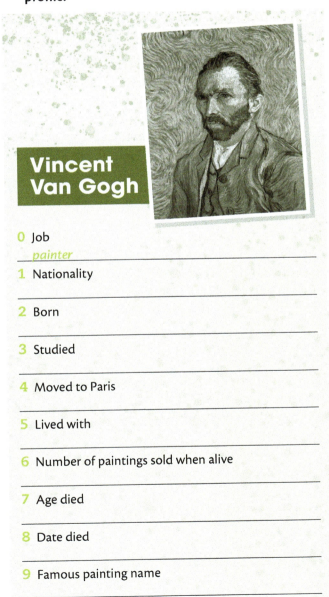

Vincent Van Gogh

0 Job
painter
1 Nationality
_____
2 Born
_____
3 Studied
_____
4 Moved to Paris
_____
5 Lived with
_____
6 Number of paintings sold when alive
_____
7 Age died
_____
8 Date died
_____
9 Famous painting name
_____

CONSOLIDATION

🎧 LISTENING

1 🔊 **10.06** **Listen to Charlotte and Jack and circle the correct answers (A, B, or C).**

1 For breakfast, Charlotte doesn't want …
   A orange juice.
   B cereal.
   C eggs.
2 Charlotte arrived home at …
   A eleven o'clock.
   B twelve o'clock.
   C one o'clock.
3 Charlotte wants to read her …
   A emails.
   B newspaper.
   C tablet.

2 🔊 **10.06** **Listen again. Mark the sentences T (true) or F (false).**

1 Charlotte wants yogurt for breakfast. ☐
2 She wants tea. ☐
3 Last night, Charlotte was at a party. ☐
4 Jack worked for five hours last night. ☐
5 Jack says he always works hard. ☐
6 The weather is rainy and cold. ☐
7 Charlotte wants to borrow Jack's tablet. ☐
8 Charlotte is going to work. ☐

Ⓖ GRAMMAR

3 Circle the correct options.

1 Dad, *can / must* I ask you a question?
2 Hurry up! We *must / mustn't* be late again.
3 Are you hungry? *Would / Do* you like some cake?
4 *It / There* wasn't a nice day yesterday. It was cold and rainy.
5 You really *can / must* be careful, John. Don't break it!
6 *Would / Do* you like this song?
7 *It / There* was a good basketball game on TV last night.
8 *I like / I'd like* a glass of water, please.
9 My brother *wasn't / weren't* at school yesterday.
10 I *study / studied* for the test last night.

4 Complete the sentences with the correct form of verbs from the list.

> arrive | be (x2) | like | not be (x2) | rain
> show | stay | travel | want | watch

> Our vacation last year wasn't very good! We
> ¹_____ to Ohio by car. We ²_____ very late,
> and the man at the hotel ³_____ angry with us.
> Then he ⁴_____ us the rooms. They ⁵_____
> really small and cold. We ⁶_____ to change the
> rooms, but the man said that there ⁷_____ any
> other rooms. We ⁸_____ in the hotel for three
> nights. The weather ⁹_____ good. It ¹⁰_____
> almost all the time! One day, I stayed in my room and
> ¹¹_____ TV for about six hours. But the food was
> good. We ¹²_____ it a lot. Next year, we don't
> want to go to that hotel again.

🔤 VOCABULARY

5 Complete the words.

1 Do you want black coffee or coffee with m _ _ k?
2 It's cold and w _ _ _ y today.
3 I don't eat a lot of v _ _ _ _ _ _ _ _ s.
4 My favorite fruit is an o _ _ _ _ _ _ .
5 I was at home yesterday e _ _ _ _ _ g.
6 It was her birthday last M _ _ _ h.
7 There's no sun today – it's very c _ _ _ _ y.
8 I watched tennis yesterday a _ _ _ _ _ _ _ _ n.
9 I'd like apple juice and eggs for b _ _ _ _ _ _ _ t.
10 I love eating b _ _ _ _ _ s and fries.

6 Complete the dialogue with words from the list.

> dinner | fruit | meat | night | o'clock
> potatoes | strawberries | tea

Liam What time do you usually eat in your family?
Nicky Well, we usually have lunch at one ⁰_____ *o'clock* _____ .
And then we have ¹_____ at eight in the evening.
Liam And what do you eat in the evening?
Nicky We have ²_____ – beef or chicken – and some vegetables, like carrots or ³_____ . I usually drink juice, but my parents like hot drinks, so they have ⁴_____ .
Liam And then?
Nicky Then we have ⁵_____ , usually apples, but last ⁶_____ we had ⁷_____ – they're my favorite!

DIALOGUE

7 🔊 **10.07** **Complete the dialogue with the words from the list. There are two extra words. Then listen and check.**

> bit | can | careful | course | liked | mustn't | thing | wanted | was | wasn't | were | weren't

Clara So, what was Jason's party like last night?

Giorgio It was great. We all enjoyed it. There ¹_____ great music, and I danced a lot. And all my friends were there.

Clara Was there any food?

Giorgio Yes. There ²_____ sandwiches and cheese and some really nice chicken wings, too. The ³_____ is …

Clara Yes?

Giorgio Well, Jason's mom cooked some risotto, and it ⁴_____ good at all! No one ⁵_____ it. At the end of the party, it was all still there! I usually love risotto, but not that!

Clara Oh, dear. Oh, look. Jason's coming. Be ⁶_____! We ⁷_____ say anything about the risotto, OK?

Giorgio No, sure. Jason! Hi. How are you? Thanks for the party!

Jason Hi, Giorgio. Hi, Clara. No problem. I'm happy that you enjoyed it. But Giorgio, ⁸_____ I ask you something?

Giorgio Uh, of ⁹_____. What?

Jason My mom's risotto. Was it really terrible? No one ¹⁰_____ to eat it!

Clara Go on, Giorgio. I think you can tell him!

📖 READING

8 **Read Emily's email. Then correct the sentences.**

1 Yesterday was Emily's fourteenth birthday.
_____

2 The restaurant only serves Chinese food.
_____

3 The restaurant was noisy.
_____

4 Emily didn't like the soup.
_____

5 Emily's mother and father don't eat fish.
_____

6 Emily's family eat in restaurants a lot.
_____

7 There was writing on the candles.
_____

8 Emily's family is having dessert at a restaurant tonight.
_____

✏️ WRITING

9 **Write a paragraph about a good or bad meal you remember. Write about 60 words. Use the questions to help you.**

- Where were you?
- What was the meal? (dinner? lunch?)
- Who was there?
- What was the food?
- Why was it a good/bad meal?

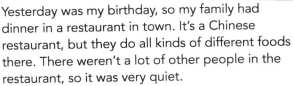

⭐ **Alli**
Emily@thinkmail.com

Hi Alli,

Yesterday was my birthday, so my family had dinner in a restaurant in town. It's a Chinese restaurant, but they do all kinds of different foods there. There weren't a lot of other people in the restaurant, so it was very quiet.

The dinner was really nice. We started with vegetable soup – it was delicious! Then I ordered beef with peppers and mushrooms. My parents ordered fish (they don't eat meat) with vegetables and rice. And for dessert, I had banana and mango ice cream, my favorite! The food was great – I enjoyed my meal a lot. We don't usually eat in restaurants, so it was a special evening.

When we finished eating, a waiter came over with a big birthday cake! It had thirteen candles on it (of course!) and the words "Happy Birthday, Emily" in big letters in the middle. The waiters and my parents started to sing "Happy Birthday to You," and the other people in the restaurant joined in, too. At the end of the song, everyone clapped – it was really nice! There was enough cake for us and the other people in the restaurant, and there's some in the fridge in our kitchen now!

So, dessert at our house tonight is birthday cake!

Love,

Emily

Grammar rap!

GRAMMAR
Simple past: irregular verbs
→ SB p.104

1 ★☆☆ **Complete the table with the simple past or the base form of the verbs.**

base form	simple past
0 ran	*ran*
1	came
2	put
3 give	
4 see	
5	knew
6	drank
7 fall	
8 write	
9	took
10 eat	

2 ★★☆ **Complete the text with the simple past form of the verbs in parentheses.**

The Hill family's vacation

Last year, the Hill family from Utah decided to go on vacation in Arizona. They ⁰___went___ (go) to northern Arizona. Mr. Hill ¹_____ (make) a reservation at a hotel in Sedona. In Sedona, they ²_____ (see) beautiful rock formations. Then Mandy ³_____ (find) Out of Africa Wildlife Park on her computer. She ⁴_____ (tell) her parents about the park with lions, zebras, and a lot of other animals. The website ⁵_____ (say) the park had hundreds of animals. The whole family ⁶_____ (think) it was a good idea to visit the park. So they ⁷_____ (get) in the car and ⁸_____ (drive) to the park. They ⁹_____ (have) a really good time there!

Simple past (negative)
→ SB p.104

3 ★★★ **Write sentences about a birthday party. Use the simple past negative.**

0 my grandmother / to the party (come)
My grandmother didn't come to the party.

1 the band / classical music (play)
_____

2 we / bread and butter (eat)
_____

3 Adriana / me a dictionary (give)
_____

4 Mom / my dress (make)
_____

5 Rob / a spider on the table (see)
_____

6 my father / us home (take)
_____

7 Stefan / a snake in a box (find)
_____

8 we / a movie (watch)
_____

4 ★★☆ **Logan didn't have a good weekend. Complete the sentences with the simple past form of the verbs in the list.**

> be | be | decide | do | not do | not rain
> not work | rain | try | use | want

0 Last weekend _____*was*_____ awful.
1 It _____ all day on Saturday.
2 I _____ anything interesting.
3 I _____ to watch a movie, but the download _____ .
4 My brother _____ the computer for his homework all afternoon.
5 I _____ to go out, but it was too cold and wet.
6 But, it _____ on Sunday. Great!
7 So I _____ to ride my bike to the park.
8 But my bike _____ broken.
9 What _____ you _____ last weekend?

5 ★★★ **Complete the text with the simple past form of a verb in the box.**

> eat | go | go | have | not be | not like
> not want | not watch | see | share | spend | take

Sarah 0 _____went_____ to Boston last weekend with three friends. They stayed in a student hotel. It was very cheap, but the rooms 1 _____ very nice. Sarah 2 _____ a room with Lisa. The hotel had a café, and on Friday evening, they 3 _____ there because they were tired from the trip. But Craig and Alex 4 _____ the pizza very much. On Saturday morning, Sarah and Alex 5 _____ to the Museum of Natural History in Cambridge. They 6 _____ a dodo and some dinosaurs. Craig and Lisa 7 _____ to look at animals, so they 8 _____ the morning in the Museum of Science instead. In the evening, they 9 _____ the subway to the theater district, but they 10 _____ a show because the tickets were very expensive. So they 11 _____ burgers, and this time, the boys were happy!

Simple past (questions) → SB p.105

6 ★★★ **Use the information in Exercise 5 and write questions about Sarah for these answers.**

0 A _Where did Sarah go last weekend?_
  B She went to Boston.
1 A Where _____
  B In a hotel.
2 A What _____ on Friday?
  B A pizza in the café.
3 A Where _____
  B In the Museum of Natural History.
4 A What _____
  B A dodo and some dinosaurs.
5 A What _____
  B A burger.

PRONUNCIATION
Short vowel sound /ʊ/ Go to page 121.

could / couldn't (ability) → SB p.107

7 ★★☆ **Last year, Ben broke his leg, and they put it in a cast. What could he do? What couldn't he do? Use phrases from the list.**

> do his homework | eat a pizza | go swimming
> listen to music | ~~play soccer~~ | play the guitar
> ride a bike | text his friends | ~~watch TV~~

0 _Ben could watch TV._
0 _He couldn't play soccer._
1 He _____
2 He _____
3 He _____
4 He _____
5 He _____
6 He _____
7 He _____

GET IT RIGHT!

Simple past
We always use the base form of the verb after **didn't** (in negative sentences) or **Did** (in questions).

✓ I didn't go to the party last Saturday.
✗ ~~I didn't went to the party last Saturday.~~
✓ Did you visit the museum?
✗ ~~Did you visited the museum?~~

Correct the sentences.

0 He didn't finished his homework.
  He didn't finish his homework.
1 Jack didn't liked the party.
  _____
2 We didn't paid much for lunch at the zoo yesterday.
  _____
3 Did they enjoyed their vacation?
  _____
4 We didn't knew where it was, but finally we found it.
  _____
5 Billy's friend didn't ate a lot of food yesterday.
  _____
6 Did you went to the party?
  _____

VOCABULARY
Verb and noun pairs

→ SB p.104

1 ★★☆ **Read the sentences. Are the underlined words correct (✓) or incorrect (✗)? Write the correct words.**

0 I always <u>do</u> my homework. ✓
_____

0 I <u>do</u> a shower every morning. ✗
_*take*_____

1 I'm tired. Let's <u>take</u> a break now. ☐
_____

2 We just <u>went</u> the shopping for the party. ☐
_____

3 Try not to <u>do</u> a lot of mistakes. ☐
_____

4 Please don't <u>make</u> too much noise when you come back. ☐
_____

5 We <u>made</u> some great photos on vacation. ☐
_____

6 Did you <u>do</u> a good time at the party? ☐
_____

2 ★★☆ **Complete the sentences with the correct verb in the correct form.**

0 They _____*went*_____ skiing last winter.

1 I always _____ excited the day before my birthday.

2 I always _____ something on the weekend. I never stay at home.

3 We live near an airport – the planes _____ a lot of noise every day.

4 Our weekend was fantastic! We _____ a party at our house.

5 Every day, when I wake up, I _____ a bath.

6 We weren't hungry so we didn't _____ breakfast.

7 _____ you always _____ the bus to school?

Adjectives

→ SB p.107

3 ★★☆ **Put the letters in order to make adjectives. Then look at the pictures and write the phrases.**

ovllye   marst   tydri   putdis   regnoudas   blehirro   gluy   teulauibf   tersniginet   lance

0 _*a lovely gorilla*_ **1** _____ **2** _____ **3** _____ **4** _____ **5** _____ **6** _____ **7** _____ **8** _____ **9** _____

4 ★★☆ **Complete the crossword and the sentences with the same words. What's the mystery word?**

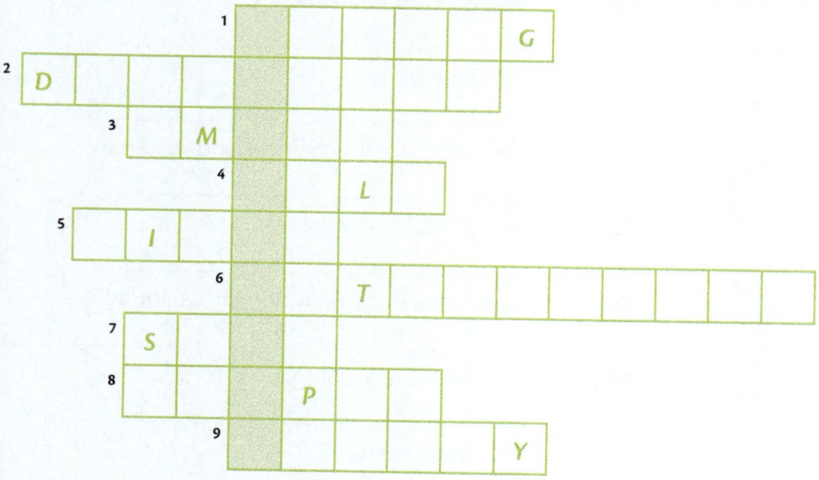

[Crossword grid]
1 ... G
2 D ...
3 M
4 L
5 I
6 T ...
7 S
8 P
9 Y

1 I don't like this movie; it's really _____ .

2 Snakes can sometimes be _____ .

3 Cats are very _____ animals.

4 I don't like that house. I think it's _____ .

5 I have to wash my parents' car because it's very _____ .

6 The class today was great. It was really _____ .

7 Some big cities aren't very _____ at night.

8 Hey! That was a really _____ thing to do!

9 Thank you for my _____ birthday present.

Mystery word: _____

REFERENCE

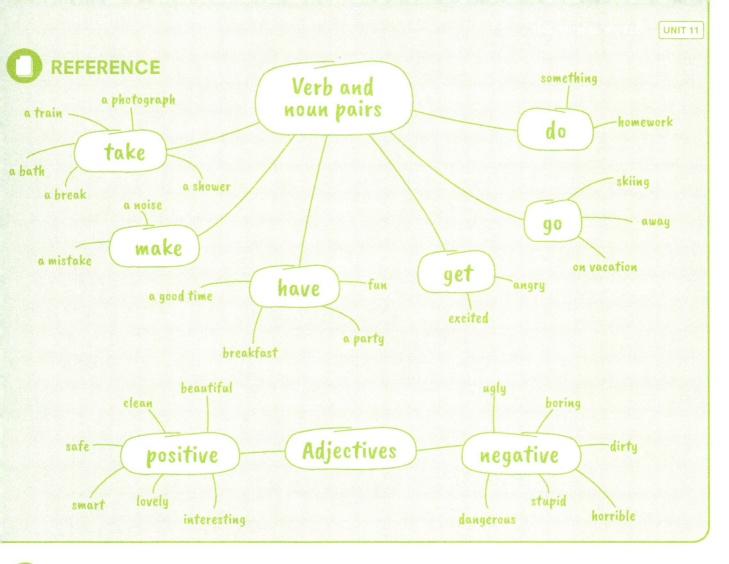

Verb and noun pairs

take
- a train
- a photograph
- a bath
- a break
- a shower

make
- a noise
- a mistake

have
- a good time
- fun
- breakfast
- a party

get
- angry
- excited

do
- something
- homework

go
- skiing
- away
- on vacation

Adjectives

positive
- clean
- beautiful
- safe
- smart
- lovely
- interesting

negative
- ugly
- boring
- dirty
- stupid
- dangerous
- horrible

VOCABULARY *EXTRA*

1 Match the verb–noun combinations from the list with the definitions.

> do nothing | get upset | go fishing
> go to bed | have dinner | make friends

0 lie down to sleep _____*go to bed*_____

1 meet new people to hang out with _____

2 feel bad about something, like losing your phone _____

3 activity in a river or the ocean _____

4 eat in the evening _____

5 you sit in your room or on the sofa and relax _____

2 Complete the sentences using the past form of the verbs and nouns in Exercise 1.

0 At Ali's new school, everyone was friendly, and he ____*made friends*____ quickly.

1 Yesterday, I had a lot of homework, and I _____ at midnight!

2 Yesterday, they _____ at the new Italian restaurant.

3 Last Sunday, we stayed at home and _____ all day. It was really boring.

4 My mom and I _____ today. We caught lots to eat for dinner.

5 My parents _____ because my sister lost her free bus pass again.

Willie the parrot

Meagan Howard and her parrot Willie shared a house in Colorado with Samantha Kuusk and Samantha's two-year-old daughter, Hannah. Meagan looked after Hannah when Samantha had school. One morning, Meagan, Willie, and Hannah were in the kitchen. Meagan made Hannah's favorite breakfast, a hot cookie. She put it on the table for a minute because it was still too hot to eat and went to the bathroom. Suddenly, Willie made a loud noise. He made sounds to say "Mama!" and "Baby!" again and again. Meagan ran back to the kitchen and saw Hannah with half of the cookie in her hand. Her face was blue and she couldn't breathe! Meagan didn't panic. She knew a special way to hit Hannah's back and a piece of cookie flew out of Hannah's mouth. Willie (and Meagan) saved Hannah!

Before that day, Willie knew several words, including *mama*, but the word *baby* was new, and Willie never said two words together. And after that, he never did again!

READING

1 **Read the stories about two animals helping a human. Which animal was wild?**

_____

2 **Read the sentences and <u>underline</u> the incorrect information. Then write correct sentences.**

Willie and the parrot

0 Willie was Meagan's <u>daughter</u>.
   Willie was Meagan's parrot.

1 Meagan gave Hannah the hot cookie.

_____

2 Meagan was in the kitchen when Hannah ate the cookie.

_____

3 Willie often said two words together.

_____

Robert and the bear

4 Robert went for a walk with his dog.

_____

5 He was worried when he saw the bears.

_____

6 The mountain lion didn't hurt Robert.

_____

7 The bear and the lion fought for a long time.

_____

3  **Read the stories again and answer the questions.**

1 How did the animals in the stories help the humans?

2 Which animal do you think was very smart? Why?

Robert and the bear

Robert Biggs lived in Paradise, California. He often went walking near the Sequoia National Forest. One day, he went to the Whiskey Flat Trail, a beautiful walk. Robert was alone, but he enjoyed the quiet. He loved seeing animals and birds on his walks. This time, he saw a family of black bears (a mother and two young cubs) drinking at a river. Robert knew the bears because he sometimes saw them on his walks. Bears in California don't usually attack humans. Robert wasn't worried. He watched the bears playing. Then, suddenly, a mountain lion jumped on his back and bit his arm. Before Robert could fight the lion, the mother bear ran over and attacked it. An adult bear is very big and strong, and after 15 seconds, the mountain lion ran away. The bear looked Robert in the eye and walked back to her cubs. She saved Robert's life.

DEVELOPING *Writing*

A blog entry about my favorite animal

1 INPUT Read the text. Why did Rita choose to write about pandas?

MY **FAVORITE** ANIMAL: **GIANT PANDAS**

My favorite animal is the giant panda. Pandas live in mountain forests in south central China. They eat bamboo and drink water from rivers. They are my favorite animals because they look so cool. They have thick black and white fur. Giant pandas are very big, but they aren't usually aggressive. That means they don't usually attack people or other animals. They are also very lazy!

In the 1960s, the Chinese government opened some panda reserves – places where pandas and the bamboo they eat are safe – because wild pandas were in danger. In these reserves, there are doctors and experts to take care of baby pandas. Because of this work, there are now nearly 1,860 wild pandas in China. The WWF organization (the World Wide Fund for Nature) has the panda as its symbol, because everyone thinks pandas are cute!

2 ANALYZE Put the headings in the order you find this information in the text.

☐ What pandas eat and drink
☐ What pandas look like
☐ Other interesting information
1 Where pandas live
☐ Why pandas are Rita's favorite animal

3 Complete the sentences with *but* or *because*.

1 Pandas are very big, _____ they aren't aggressive.
2 WWF use a panda symbol _____ everyone all around the world thinks they're cute.
3 Experts help pandas with their babies _____ the pandas have problems.
4 Pandas were in danger, _____ now they aren't.
5 Some pandas get sick, _____ doctors can usually help them.
6 I like pandas _____ they look very happy.

4 PLAN Decide which animal is your favorite. Then read the questions and make notes about your animal for a blog post.

- What is your favorite animal?
- Where does it live?
- What does it eat and drink?
- What does it look like?
- Why is it your favorite animal?
- What other interesting information can you think of about it?

✎ WRITING TIP: Using a model text

Before you write your own text, read the model text and look for any useful words or phrases you can use.

- *My favorite animal is the …*
- *They are my favorite animals because they …*

5 PRODUCE Use your notes and the text from Exercise 1 and write a blog post about your favorite animal. Write about 80 words.

🎧 LISTENING

1 🔊 **11.02** **Listen to Holly talking about volunteering at an animal rescue center. Check (✓) the animals that she talks about.**

2 🔊 **11.02** **Listen again. Mark the sentences T (true) or F (false).**

0 The boy writes for the school website. [T]

1 Holly volunteers at the Rescue Center after school. ☐

2 She couldn't work at the center when she was 14. ☐

3 They get lots of different pets at the center. ☐

4 Holly liked all the jobs she did at the center. ☐

5 The police found the snake in the police station. ☐

6 Holly loves all animals. ☐

7 Holly wants to work in a zoo when she finishes school. ☐

8 There are some wild animals at the center. ☐

DIALOGUE

3 **Complete the conversation with words and phrases from the list.**

after that | and | because
but | Poor you | Then

Adriana Did you have a good weekend?

Paulo Yes, it was great, thanks. I went to Miguel's party.

Adriana Oh, right. He invited me, too, ⁰ _____but_____ I couldn't go.

Paulo Why not?

Adriana My aunt and uncle were here for the weekend, ¹ _____ they wanted to take us out.

Paulo That's nice. Where did you go?

Adriana We went to the movies. It was really boring.

Paulo ² _____ !

Adriana But ³ _____ we went and had pizza. That was good! ⁴ _____ I ordered an enormous ice cream. I couldn't eat it all, I was so full.

Paulo That's like me at the party. I couldn't dance ⁵ _____ I was really tired from soccer on Saturday!

4 **Read the conversation again and answer the questions.**

1 Why couldn't Adriana go to the party?

_____

2 Why couldn't Adriana eat all the ice cream?

_____

3 Why couldn't Paulo dance at the party?

_____

PHRASES FOR FLUENCY → SB p.108

5 **Put the letters in order to make expressions.**

0 dunylsed ...   _suddenly ..._

1 lal thrig.   _____

2 opor oyu!   _____

3 thwa phedapen?   _____

6 **Complete the conversation with the expressions in Exercise 1.**

Eva Do you know what happened to me last weekend?

Katya No, of course not. I wasn't with you last weekend. ⁰ _What happened?_

Eva ¹ _____ , I'll tell you. On Saturday, I was in the café on Main Street, and ² _____ someone waved at me!

Katya So? Who was it?

Eva It was Jenny Hall.

Katya Jenny Hall? Are you sure? Jenny's in the UK! She moved last year.

Eva Well, she's here on vacation. But it was awful.

Katya Why?

Eva I couldn't remember her name! I called her Annie. And she got really angry with me! She shouted at me!

Katya Oh, ³ _____ . I'm sure that was horrible for you!

SUM IT UP

BACK-IN-TIME TRAVEL

Welcome to the wonderful world of Back-in-Time Travel.

As you know, last year the famous Professor Reddy of Bangalore University invented the **Back-in-Time Travel Machine**.

Now, you can go into the past! (Sorry, no future travel yet – maybe next year?)

Sit in the Back-in-Time, choose your time in the past – and whoosh! Off you go!

We are offering one-day trips to the past for only $1,000,000 USD! That's right! Only a million dollars for 24 hours in a past time period that you choose.

But here's some really good news – we have a competition, and the five winners will get a free one-day trip in the Back-in-Time!

All you have to do is write to say what time in the past you want to travel to and why. Write between 10 and 20 words, beginning with "I want to go to …" Here are two examples to help you:

"I want to go to prehistoric times and see the dinosaurs because they're fantastic animals!" (Frieda, Germany)

"I want to go to 2006 because that's when my country won the World Cup, but I wasn't alive then!" (Bruno, Italy)

But remember – if you win, you must go to the time you wrote about!

Send your ideas to us at: Back-in-Time Travel, P.O. Box 2020, London

Talk to William Shakespeare!

See the dinosaurs!

Watch the Egyptians building the pyramids!

1 Read the advertisement. Mark the sentences T (true) or F (false).

1 A man in New York invented the travel machine. ☐
2 You can travel to the past and into the future. ☐
3 You can buy a trip into the past for one million US dollars. ☐
4 The time trips are for one day. ☐
5 Five people can win a prize in the competition. ☐
6 If you win, you can go to any time in the past you want. ☐

2 Imagine there's a time machine. Where would you like to go? Write an entry for the competition.

- Say what time in the past you want to travel to and why.
- Write a paragraph, beginning with "I want to go to …"

12 MOVING AROUND

Grammar rap!

GRAMMAR
Comparative adjectives
→ SB p.112

1 ⭐☆☆ **Underline the comparative adjective in each sentence.**

0 The train is <u>faster</u> than the car.

1 His bicycle is more expensive than my bicycle.

2 Surfing is more dangerous than tennis.

3 The weather in the winter is worse than in the summer.

4 Spanish is easier than Chinese.

5 Your phone is better than my phone.

6 My house is further from school than your house.

7 Their car is bigger than our car.

8 Salad is healthier than fries.

2 ⭐☆☆ **Complete the table with the correct adjective forms.**

adjective	comparative
0 dirty	*dirtier*
1 beautiful	
2 cold	
3	curlier
4 hot	
5	cleaner
6	shorter
7 ugly	
8	more boring
9 sad	
10 warm	
11 lovely	
12	slower
13	more interesting

3 ⭐⭐☆ **Look at the table and mark the sentences T (true) or F (false). Correct the false sentences.**

	Leaves Boston	Arrives Washington, D.C.	Price
train	8 a.m.	1 p.m.	$140
bus	5 a.m.	5 p.m.	$35
plane	10 a.m.	11:30 a.m.	$75

0 The train is cheaper than the bus. ⬚ F
The train is more expensive than the bus.

1 The bus arrives later than the train. ⬚
_____

2 The bus is slower than the plane. ⬚
_____

3 The bus is more expensive than the plane. ⬚
_____

4 The plane is faster than the train. ⬚
_____

5 The plane arrives earlier than the bus. ⬚
_____

4 ⭐⭐⭐ **Use the table in Exercise 3 to write sentences. Use comparative adjectives.**

0 bus / early / train
The bus leaves earlier than the train.

1 train / fast / bus
_____

2 plane / expensive / bus
_____

3 train / slow / plane
_____

4 bus / late / plane
_____

5 bus / cheap / train
_____

PRONUNCIATION
Word stress – comparatives
Go to page 121.

5 ★★★ **Look at the pictures and write sentences to compare the two taxi companies. Use the adjectives in the list to help you.**

> big | clean | dangerous | dirty
> expensive | fast | good | safe

0 *Lidia's limos are cleaner than Tim's taxis.*
1 _____
2 _____
3 _____
4 _____
5 _____
6 _____
7 _____

6 ★★★ **Complete the sentences so they are true for you.**

1 I'm _____ than my parents.
2 My best friend is _____ than me.
3 English classes are _____ than math classes.
4 Parrots are _____ than cats.
5 Summer is _____ than winter.
6 Walking is _____ than cycling.

one / ones

→ SB p.115

7 ★☆☆ (Circle) **the correct options.**

0 Can I have a look at those jeans? The *one* / (*ones*) in the window.
1 Don't buy me a coffee. I don't want *one* / *ones*.
2 I like most movies, but I don't like *one* / *ones* about war.
3 I can't give you a piece of paper because I don't have *one* / *ones*.
4 I have some apples. Would you like *one* / *ones*?
5 I'm interested in cars, and I really like Italian *one* / *ones*.

8 ★★☆ **Write *one* into the dialogues in the correct place.**

0 A Where's your house?

                                   one
   B My house is the first ˅ on the left.

1 A How was your birthday?

   B Great. I got a lot of presents, but my favorite was a book from my dad.

2 A Which dress did you buy?

   B Well, I love red, so I bought the red.

3 A How is your new computer?

   B It's faster than my old, and it's easier to use.

4 A Is that your cousin over there?

   B Yes, he's the with the glasses.

GET IT RIGHT!

one and ones

We use *one* or *ones* after an adjective when we want to avoid repeating a noun.

✓ *I like this song; it's a good one.*
✗ *I like this song; it's a good song.*
✓ *I wore my new shoes – the red ones.*
✗ *I wore my new shoes – the red shoes.*

Replace one of the nouns with *one* or *ones*.

0 How much are the cakes? I mean the big cakes.
   How much are the cakes? I mean the big ones.
1 These tickets are expensive. We can find cheaper tickets.
   _____
2 This pen isn't good. I have a better pen in my bag.
   _____
3 The blue jeans are too big. The black jeans are much better.
   _____
4 All of the buses go there, but the red bus is the fastest.
   _____
5 Where are my black shoes? They were next to my brown shoes.
   _____

VOCABULARY
Transportation

→ SB p.112

1 ★☆☆ Find and circle five more types of transportation in the word snake.

agemotorcycleasehelicoptermmbdplanerkutaxilfqferryipatrainbgh

2 ★★☆ Put the letters in order to make the column titles. Then complete the table with words from Exercise 1.

no het ardo	no sairl	ni eth ria	no tware
0 _on the road_	1 _____	2 _____	3 _____
motorcycle			

3 ★★★ Match the words from Exercise 1 with their definitions.

0 It flies in the air, but it doesn't have wings. _____helicopter_____

1 It travels on rails and is very long. _____

2 It flies in the air. It has wings. _____

3 It travels on water and carries a lot of people. _____

4 You pay someone to drive you. _____

5 It drives on the road but only has two wheels. _____

Geographical places

→ SB p.115

4 ★★☆ Find the places in the word search. Write the words under the pictures.

Q	H	C	A	E	B	W	W	M
H	E	E	O	F	G	S	O	S
F	V	S	U	D	R	U	R	E
O	M	C	D	U	N	A	K	R
R	H	R	R	T	B	A	E	U
E	T	P	A	B	L	V	S	C
S	X	I	E	F	I	P	B	T
T	N	C	K	R	R	T	D	B
Z	D	L	E	I	F	C	O	V

forest

_____

_____

_____

_____

_____

_____

5 ★★☆ Match the geographical places with the famous examples.

1 mountain ☐
2 lake ☐
3 river ☐
4 beach ☐
5 ocean ☐

a The Nile, The Amazon, The Yangtze
b Aconcagua, K2, Kilimanjaro
c Copacabana, Bondi, Kuta
d Atlantic, Pacific, Indian
e Michigan, Titicaca, Victoria

6 ★★★ Complete the sentences with examples from your own country.

1 My favorite beach is _____.
2 The highest mountain is _____.
3 A famous lake is _____.
4 The longest river is _____.
5 _____ is a good place to go on vacation.
6 _____ is a beautiful place in the winter.

REFERENCE

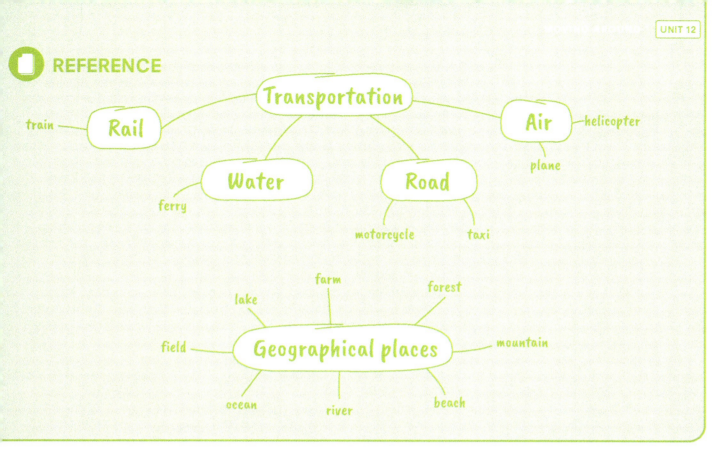

VOCABULARY *EXTRA*

1 Label the pictures of day and night with the words from the list.

cloud | moon | sky | star | sun

1 _____
2 _____
3 _____

4 _____
5 _____

2 Choose the correct answers (A, B, or C).

1 The color of the sky is really _____ .
  A blue   B red   C no color
2 The sun is _____ million kilometers from our planet.
  A 98.7   B 149.6   C 203.5
3 A cloud is _____ .
  A air with water or ice in it   B hot   C water or ice
4 The Moon goes around the Earth every _____ .
  A 30.25 days   B 29.98 days   C 27.32 days
5 There are about _____ stars in the universe.
  A 1 billion   B 1 trillion   C 1 billion trillion

Answers: 1 A – We see blue light because of air molecules; 2 B; 3 A; 4 C; 5 C (very approximately)

RACING
AROUND THE
WORLD!

My favorite book is called *Around the World in 80 Days*. It's the story of a man who makes a bet that he can travel around the planet in less than 80 days. Of course, these days that's not difficult, but the book is set more than 100 years ago. I love the idea of adventure and exploring, so it's no surprise that my favorite TV show is called *The Amazing Race*. It's an American reality show, and it's really exciting. On the show, teams race against each other around the world to win a big prize. There are two people on each team, like a husband and wife, a father and son, best friends, etc. It's important that they have a good relationship because the race is really difficult and they need to be strong and help each other.

The race takes them all over the world, and they use lots of different types of transportation. They use planes, of course, to make the longer journeys, but they also use boats, taxis, buses, helicopters, bikes, cars, trains – any transportation that makes their journey quicker.

At the beginning of each show, the host tells the teams where they have to go. The last team to arrive at that place leaves the show. When there are only three teams left, they race to the final place. The team that arrives first usually wins lots of money.

I love this show because you see lots of really exciting places all over the world. One day, I want to be on the show.

READING

1 Read the blog. Which of these types of transportation is <u>not</u> mentioned?

2 Read the blog again and match the sentence halves.

0 *Around the World in 80 Days*   g
1 *The Amazing Race* ☐
2 The race is ☐
3 The people on the teams ☐
4 The teams race ☐
5 The teams use ☐
6 The last team to arrive ☐
7 In the final ☐
8 The winning team ☐

a between teams of two people.
b all over the world.
c leaves the show.
d gets a lot of money.
e is a TV show from the US.
f a lot of different types of transportation.
g is a famous book.
h know each other.
i there are three teams.

3 CRITICAL THINKING Do you want to be on *The Amazing Race*? Why or why not? Write a short paragraph (60–80 words).

DEVELOPING *Writing*

Writing about a trip

1 **INPUT** Read about Eric and Alexia's favorite trips. Do they prefer leaving or coming home?

Eric

My favorite trip is the one I make every Saturday morning to play basketball. I leave my house at about nine o'clock and get on my bike to bike the three kilometers to the sports club. It takes me about 15 minutes. At the club, I meet my team, and we play a game. Then I get on my bike and ride back home. I like the trip there because I get excited about playing basketball. I don't like the trip back so much because I'm usually very tired. But when I have a good game, the trip back is great, too, because I think about the game.

Alexia

The trip I like best is the one from my house to my dad's house. My dad lives in Texas, and three times every year, I fly there to spend some time with him. The trip starts really early. The taxi picks me up from my house at 4 a.m.! But that's OK, because I'm always really happy. It's only 30 minutes to the airport, but I can't wait to get there. The plane trip is about four hours. It's not very exciting, but I usually listen to music or go to sleep. My dad always meets me at the airport, and then he drives me to his house. We don't stop talking the whole trip. I never like the trip back. I'm always really sad to leave.

2 **ANALYZE** Read the texts again and complete the table.

	from	to	transportation	time it takes	why I like it
Eric					
Alexia					

3 **PLAN** Think about your favorite trip and make notes to complete the table so it is true for you.

	from	to	transportation	time	why I like it
Me					

4 **PRODUCE** Use your notes to write a text about your favorite trip. Write 35–50 words.

✎ WRITING TIP: Useful language

- *My favorite trip is the one I make* (every Saturday morning) *to* (play basketball).
- *The trip I like best is the one from* (my house) *to* (my dad's house).
- *The trip starts* (really early).
- *It takes me about* (15 minutes).
- *I like the trip there because* (I get excited about playing basketball.)
- *I don't like the trip back* (so much) *because* (I'm usually very tired).

🎧 LISTENING

1 🔊 **12.02** Listen to the conversation. Where is Jill? Who is she talking to?

_____

2 🔊 **12.02** Listen again and ⟨circle⟩ the correct answers (A, B, or C).

0 Where does Jill want to go?

  A Washington, D.C.

  Ⓑ New York

  C Boston

1 What time is the next train?

  A

  B

  C

2 How often is there a train?

  A every 15 minutes

  B every 30 minutes

  C every 50 minutes

3 How long is the trip?

  A 40 minutes

  B 35 minutes

  C 45 minutes

4 When is Jill returning?

  A today

  B tomorrow

  C on the weekend

5 How much is the ticket?

  A $7.80

  B $8.70

  C $17.80

6 What platform is the train leaving from?

  A 3

  B 4

  C 5

7 What time does Jill get the train?

  A

  B

  C

DIALOGUE

3 ⟨Circle⟩ the correct options. Then put the conversation in order.

☐	**Assistant**	The trip is ¹*a quarter / half* of an hour.
☐	**Assistant**	OK, that's $7.80, please.
☐	**Assistant**	Platform 5. Have a ²*good / boring* trip.
☐	**Assistant**	Let me see. There's a train every 15 minutes, so the next one is at three thirty.
☐	**Assistant**	Do you want one-way ticket or a round-trip ticket?
1	**Assistant**	Good afternoon. ³*How / Who* can I help you?
☐	**Woman**	That's great. And how long does it take?
☐	**Woman**	Thank you.
☐	**Woman**	I want to ⁴*go / come* to New York. What time's the next train?
☐	**Woman**	Just one more thing. What platform does the train leave ⁵*from / at*?
☐	**Woman**	30 minutes. That's fast. Can I have a ticket, please?
☐	**Woman**	A round-trip ticket, please. I'm coming back later.

Train to TH!NK

Comparing

4 Complete the diagram with the words from the list. Then use your own ideas and write six more words.

> boring | dangerous | exciting
> expensive | fun | relaxing

5 Write sentences to compare the two different

Vacations by the ocean

Vacations in the mountains

types of vacations in Exercise 4.

_____
_____
_____

TOWARDS A2 Key for Schools

EXAM SKILLS: READING
Answering open cloze questions

1 Read Matteo's answers in the task below. How many did he get right? How many did he get wrong?

Complete the text about travelling to and from school. Write ONE word for each space.

I live ⁰_____*in*_____ a small town and my school is about six kilometres away. Most days I take the school bus. It stops outside my house ¹_____*at*_____ 7.30 every morning. In the summer, when the weather ²_____*are*_____ good, I usually cycle to school. It's quicker ³_____*than*_____ the bus because the bus stops all the time. The problem with the bike is when my school bag is too heavy. Then it's ⁴_____*not*_____ fun. Sometimes I wake up late and ⁵_____*mis*_____ the school bus. Mum takes me to school ⁶_____*in*_____ the car. She doesn't like this ⁷_____*because*_____ she needs to get to work, too. Once I missed the bus home and I had to ⁸_____*tired*_____ home. It took me more than ⁹_____*half an*_____ hour to walk. I don't want ¹⁰_____*to*_____ do that again.

✏️ READING TIP:

- Read the instructions carefully. Underline the key words. Words like *circle*, *tick*, *choose* and *underline* tell you how to complete the question. Look for other important information, for example, *Write ONE word for each space.*
- When you have finished, read your answers again. Have you followed the instructions? Have you used the correct type of word (verb, noun, adjective, etc.)? Have you used the singular and plural forms correctly? Is your spelling correct?
- Don't leave any gaps. If you don't know the answer, guess!

2 Put Matteo's mistakes under the correct heading. Write the number.

Used more than one word	Used the wrong type of word (adjective instead of verb)	Used singular and plural forms incorrectly	Used incorrect spelling
9			

3 Correct Matteo's mistakes. Write the correct words next to the numbers in Exercise 2.

4 Complete the text about favourite holidays. Write ONE word for each space.

My favourite holidays ⁰_____*are*_____ beach holidays. I like the sun ¹_____ the sea. I usually go on beach holidays ²_____ the summer with my family. Sometimes Dad drives and sometimes we ³_____ the train. Last year, we went ⁴_____ holiday in the countryside. We stayed on ⁵_____ farm. There was a river and a lake and lots ⁶_____ fields, too. It was OK, but I prefer beach holidays. The weather by the sea is usually hotter ⁷_____ in the countryside. Dad wants to ⁸_____ on holiday in the mountains this year. I'm ⁹_____ happy about that idea. I don't want another year away ¹⁰_____ the beach.

CONSOLIDATION

🎧 LISTENING

1 🔊 **12.03** Listen to Caleb and ⓒircle the correct answers (A, B, or C).

1 How old is Caleb's brother?
   A eight   B nine   C ten
2 At the zoo, which animals scared Caleb's brother?
   A the elephants   B the lions   C the tigers
3 How many jaguars were there?
   A two   B three   C four

2 🔊 **12.03** Listen again and answer the questions.

1 Why did Caleb's family go to the zoo?
_____

2 Who took photos at the zoo?
_____

3 What was Caleb happy about?
_____

4 What did Caleb think about the visit to the zoo?
_____

5 Why was Caleb sorry for the jaguars?
_____

6 What two things does Caleb think zoo animals need?
_____

ⓖ GRAMMAR

3 Complete the sentences with the correct form of the words in parentheses.

1 Yesterday, I _____ some money on the street. (find)
2 For my last birthday, my parents _____ me tickets for a concert. (give)
3 My friends and I _____ to the movies three times last month. (go)
4 I arrived home late last night, but I _____ any noise. (not make)
5 Yesterday's test was _____ than the one on Friday. (difficult)
6 _____ you _____ that movie on TV last Sunday night? (see)
7 The weather today is _____ than yesterday. (bad)
8 I practice a lot, and I'm getting _____ every day! (good)
9 I _____ many presents for my birthday. (not get)
10 Are tigers _____ than jaguars? (big)

🔤 VOCABULARY

4 ⓒircle the odd one out in each list. Explain your reasons.

0 safe   clean   ⓗomework
   It's a noun – the other two are adjectives.

1 motorcycle   plane   helicopter
_____

2 shopping   homework   a mistake
_____

3 forest   ocean   lake
_____

4 train   river   subway
_____

5 a break   a good time photos
_____

6 boat   ferry   taxi
_____

7 a mistake   a shower   a noise
_____

8 breakfast   elephant   horse
_____

9 field   beach   farm
_____

5 Use a word or phrase from Exercise 4 to complete each sentence.

1 Shh! Don't make _____ or that pretty bird will fly away.
2 We went for a walk in the _____ this morning. The trees were very beautiful.
3 My mom doesn't like me riding my bike in the city. She thinks it isn't _____ .
4 This party's great. I'm having _____ .
5 Her name's Julie, but I made _____ and called her Jenny.
6 I like taking _____ after soccer to get clean again!
7 We went to the beach, but I didn't swim in the _____ – I think it's dangerous.
8 I'm really tired. Let's take _____ and have some coffee.

DIALOGUE

6 🔊 12.04 **Complete the dialogue with the words and phrases from the list. There are two extra words/phrases. Then listen and check.**

All right | better | came | cheaper | could | didn't | Did | lovely | made | That's terrible | suddenly | What happened

Jin How was your weekend at the beach?

Maria Oh, awful. Everything went wrong.

Jin Oh, no. ¹_____ ?

Maria Well, first, we missed the bus.

Jin But you got there in the end?

Maria Oh, yes, we got there. We always stay at the same hotel. But it's very expensive, so this year Dad said, "Let's stay at a ²_____ hotel." I said, "Dad! If our usual hotel is more expensive, that's because it's ³_____ than the cheaper ones." ⁴_____ he listen? No, he didn't. The hotel was horrible! I ⁵_____ sleep at all – there were cars outside all night. They ⁶_____ a lot of noise!

Jin ⁷_____ , but what about the beach?

Maria The beach there is really ⁸_____ . We like it a lot. So we went there on the first day – but ⁹_____ it started to rain! We ¹⁰_____ home a day early. The weekend was … well, it was horrible.

📖 READING

The Scottish Highlands – there's nowhere more beautiful!

Are you thinking about taking a break? Then try the Scottish Highlands. This lovely part of Scotland has forests, rivers, lakes – called *lochs* in Scotland – and, of course, mountains! The mountains are beautiful and quiet, with fantastic walks. Check the weather first, though, as it can change very quickly!

The town of Inverness is the capital of the Highlands. It has lots of interesting stores and restaurants. Try haggis, a Scottish speciality. You can also visit Cawdor Castle, 14 miles away. Inverness is on the coast, so there's a beach, but it can be cold, even in the summer!

Another place to see is Loch Ness, the lake famous for its monster, Nessie! Visit the museum or take a boat trip across the loch.

There are a lot of hotels and bed-and-breakfast places in the Highlands. The B&Bs are cheaper, but sometimes they're as good as hotels. The breakfasts are really big, so expect to be full all day! They often serve afternoon tea, with sandwiches and cake, too.

You can get to Inverness or Fort William by train, but to visit the lochs and the mountains, it's easier to drive.

Why not visit the Highlands soon? We'd love to see you!

7 **Read the web page. Mark the sentences T (true) or F (false).**

1 Lakes in Scotland have a different name. ☐

2 You have to check the weather before you go for a walk. ☐

3 There isn't a lot to do in Inverness. ☐

4 Loch Ness has a famous monster. ☐

5 B&Bs are more expensive than hotels. ☐

6 At the B&B places, you usually get a small breakfast. ☐

7 You can't visit everywhere in the Highlands by train. A car is better. ☐

✏️ WRITING

8 **Write a paragraph about a nice area that you know. Write 60–80 words. Use the questions to help you.**

- What is it called?
- What are the good things about it?
- What can people do there?
- How can you get there?

PRONUNCIATION

UNIT 1
/h/ or /w/ in question words

1 Look at the question words. Two of them start with the /h/ sound and the others start with the /w/ sound. Write /h/ or /w/ next to the words.

- **0** Why _____ /w/ _____
- **1** How _____
- **2** Where _____
- **3** Who _____
- **4** What _____
- **5** When _____

2 🔊 1.01 Listen, check, and repeat.

3 Match the words that rhyme.

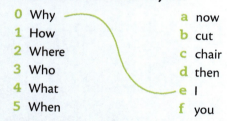

- **0** Why
- **1** How
- **2** Where
- **3** Who
- **4** What
- **5** When

- **a** now
- **b** cut
- **c** chair
- **d** then
- **e** I
- **f** you

4 🔊 1.02 Listen, check, and repeat.

UNIT 2
Vowel sounds – adjectives

1 🔊 2.01 Listen and repeat the adjectives.

angry	awful	bored	busy
friendly	funny	happy	hot
hungry	sad	thirsty	worried

2 Complete the table with the words from Exercise 1.

a (cat)	e (get)	i (six)	ah (dog)
0 angry	3 _____	4 _____	5 _____
1 _____			6 _____
2 _____			

u (bus)	or (for)	ir (bird)	
7 _____	9 _____	10 _____	
8 _____		11 _____	

3 🔊 2.02 Listen, check, and repeat.

UNIT 3
this / that / these / those

1 🔊 3.01 Listen and repeat. Then look at the underlined sounds and circle the odd sound out.

0 those	g<u>o</u>	h<u>o</u>me	⬭bored⬭
1 th<u>a</u>t	s<u>a</u>d	l<u>a</u>te	h<u>a</u>ve
2 th<u>e</u>m	th<u>e</u>se	pl<u>ea</u>se	m<u>ee</u>t
3 g<u>i</u>ve	l<u>i</u>ke	th<u>i</u>s	s<u>i</u>ng
4 h<u>o</u>t	c<u>o</u>ld	kn<u>ow</u>	th<u>o</u>se
5 w<u>i</u>fe	th<u>i</u>s	n<u>i</u>ce	exc<u>i</u>ting
6 th<u>e</u>se	sh<u>e</u>	g<u>e</u>t	w<u>e</u>
7 f<u>a</u>mous	th<u>a</u>t	m<u>a</u>tch	h<u>a</u>ppy

2 🔊 3.02 Listen again, check, and repeat.

UNIT 4
Word stress in numbers

1 🔊 **4.01** **Listen to the words and write them in the correct column according to the stress.**

> eighteen | eighty | forty | fourteen | nineteen
> ninety | sixteen | sixty | thirty | thirteen

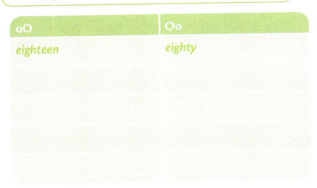

oO	Oo
eighteen	*eighty*

2 🔊 **4.01** **Listen again, check, and repeat.**

UNIT 5
Simple present verbs – third person

1 **Complete the table with the correct simple present third person singular form of the verbs in the list.**

> catch | cook | choose | dance | help | look
> sing | teach | walk | wash | watch | wish | work

one syllable	two syllables
cooks	*catches*

2 🔊 **5.01** **Listen, check, and repeat.**

UNIT 6
Long vowel sound /eɪ/

1 🔊 **6.01** **Listen to these words. They all contain the /eɪ/ sound. <u>Underline</u> the sound in each word.**

0 br<u>ea</u>k

1 eight

2 face

3 great

4 gray

5 make

6 rainy

7 say

8 straight

9 take

10 they

11 waiter

2 **Complete the sentences with the words in Exercise 1.**

0 How do you _____*say*_____ that word in English?

1 Is your grandmother the woman with the wavy _____ hair?

2 Let's _____ Clara a friendship band for her birthday!

3 My little sister is _____ years old.

4 These are my friends. _____ like playing soccer with me.

5 It's _____ today. Let's go to the movies.

6 My father's a _____ at that restaurant.

7 I brush my teeth and wash my _____ every morning.

8 I like playing tennis. It's a _____ game!

9 Can you _____ this book to your teacher? Thank you.

10 My hair's _____ , but my best friend's hair is curly.

11 Put away your books. It's time for a _____ .

3 🔊 **6.02** **Listen, check, and repeat.**

UNIT 7
Vowel sound /ɔr/

1 🔊 7.01 **Listen to these words. They all contain the /ɔr/ sound. <u>Underline</u> the sound in each word.**

0 <u>or</u>ange

1 morning

2 tour

3 door

4 forty

5 important

6 quarter

7 short

8 snowboarding

9 sport

10 store

11 floor

2 **Complete the sentences with the words in Exercise 1.**

0 Please close the _____door_____ when you go out.
1 This city is beautiful. Let's go on a _____ .
2 Please buy some food at the _____ .
3 English is a very _____ language.
4 The office is on the fourth _____ .
5 I have art class in the _____ .
6 Jenny likes _____ in the mountains in the winter.
7 My favorite _____ is volleyball.
8 I'm thirsty. Can I have a glass of _____ juice, please?
9 My hair is long, but my friend's is _____ .
10 My first class at school starts at a _____ to nine.
11 It's my father's birthday today. He's _____ years old.

3 🔊 7.02 **Listen, check, and repeat.**

UNIT 8
Intonation – listing items

1 **Complete the lists. Then draw a ↗ and a ↘ to show where intonation rises and falls in each list.**

> arm | Brazil | catch | coat | headphones | June
> library | Russian | rugby | stove | spring | wife

↗ ↗ ↗ ↘

0 March, April, May, and _____June_____

1 son, daughter, husband, and _____

2 Japanese, British, _____ , and Turkish

3 _____ , skirt, socks, and shoes

4 snowboarding, gymnastics, golf, and _____

5 summer, _____ , winter, and fall

6 watch, choose, throw, and _____

7 _____ , shower, fridge, and armchair

8 Australia, Scotland, _____ , and Japan

9 body, _____ , leg, and face

10 tablet, GPS, _____ , and laptop

11 _____ , restaurant, museum, and bank

2 🔊 8.01 **Listen, check, and repeat.**

UNIT 9
Intonation – giving two choices

1 🔊 9.01 **Complete the dialogue with the words in the list. Then listen and check.**

> chicken | fish | fries | ice cream
> pineapple | soup | tea | water

↗   ↘

Waiter	Would you like salad or ⁰___*soup*___?
Woman	Salad, please.

☐   ☐

Waiter	Chicken or ¹_____?
Woman	I think I'll have ²_____ today – with ³_____, please.
Waiter	Would you like dessert?
Woman	Yes, please.

☐   ☐

Waiter	Cake or ⁴_____?
Woman	I'd prefer fruit – some ⁵_____, please.
Waiter	Would you like something to drink?
Woman	Yes, please – just some ⁶_____. And a cup of ⁷_____ after the meal. Thank you.

2 🔊 9.01 **Draw ↗ or ↘ above the waiter's questions. Then listen, check, and repeat.**

UNIT 10
Simple past regular verbs

1 **Say the verbs in the list in the past tense and decide if they are one syllable or two. Then write the verbs in the correct column.**

> dance | hate | help | like | live | need
> play | start | wait | walk | want | work

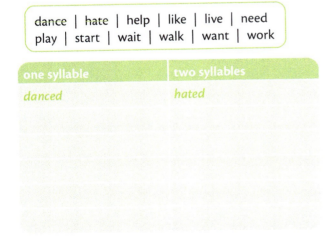

one syllable	two syllables
danced	*hated*

2 🔊 10.01 **Listen, check, and repeat.**

3 **Complete the rule.**

We only say /ɪd/ when the final sound in the word is
a / _____ / or a / _____ /.

UNIT 11
Short vowel sound /ʊ/

1 **Circle the odd sound out.**

0	(cook)	true	food
1	house	shout	could
2	June	put	who
3	room	you	woods
4	pull	fun	son
5	foot	put	jump
6	move	zoo	good
7	funny	woolly	sunny
8	two	room	book
9	push	run	bus
10	cousin	couldn't	country

2 🔊 11.01 **Listen, check, and repeat.**

UNIT 12
Word stress – comparatives

1 **Write the comparative form of the adjectives. Underline the stressed syllable.**

0	slow	*slower*	8	big	_____
1	small	_____	9	hot	_____
2	quick	_____	10	funny	_____
3	cheap	_____	11	easy	_____
4	fast	_____	12	healthy	_____
5	cold	_____	13	happy	_____
6	safe	_____	14	far	_____
7	close	_____	15	good	_____

2 🔊 12.01 **Listen, check, and repeat.**

3 **Complete the rule.**

When adding -er to make a comparative, the
first / second syllable is always stressed.

GRAMMAR REFERENCE

UNIT 1
Question words

1 Questions that begin with *Who* ask about a person/people.

Who is he?
He's the new teacher.

2 Questions that begin with *What* ask about a thing/things.

What's that?
It's a cell phone.

3 Questions that begin with *When* ask about a time/day/year, etc.

When's the soccer game?
It's at three o'clock.

4 Questions that begin with *Where* ask about a place.

Where's Cambridge?
It's in Massachusetts.

5 Questions that begin with *Why* ask for a reason.

Why are you here?
Because I want to see you.

6 Questions that begin with *How old* ask about age.

How old is she?
She's sixteen.

to be

1 The simple present of *to be* is like this:

Singular	Plural
I am	we are
you are	you are
he/she/it is	they are

2 In speaking and informal writing we use contracted (short) forms.

I'm, you're, he's, she's, it's, we're, they're
I'm from Russia.
She's late.
We're hungry.

UNIT 2
to be (negative, singular, and plural)

1 We make the verb *to be* negative by adding *not*.

Singular	Plural
I am not (I'm not)	we are not (we aren't)
you are not (you aren't)	you are not (you aren't)
he/she/it is not (he/she/it isn't)	they are not (they aren't)

I'm not Brazilian. I'm Portuguese.
He *isn't* late. He's early!
They *aren't* from Spain. They're from Mexico.

to be (questions and short answers)

To make questions with *to be*, we put the verb before the subject. We make short answers with *Yes* or *No* + subject + the verb *to be*. We don't use contracted forms in positive short answers (NOT: *Yes, you're.*)

Am I late?	Yes, you are. / No, you aren't.
Are you American?	Yes, I am. / No, I'm not.
Is he a singer?	Yes, he is. / No, he isn't.
Is she from Japan?	Yes, she is. / No, she isn't.
Are we right?	Yes, we are. / No, we aren't.
Are they French?	Yes, they are. / No, they aren't.

Object pronouns

1 Object pronouns come after a verb. We use them instead of nouns.

I like *the movie*. I like *it*.
I love *my sister*. I love *her*.
They are friends with *you and me*. They are friends with *us*.
I like *the girls at my school*. I like *them*.

2 The object pronouns are:

Subject	I	you	he	she	it	we	they
Object	me	you	him	her	it	us	them

UNIT 3

Possessive 's

1 **We use 's after a noun to say who something belongs to.**

Dad's room
John's car
Sandra's family
the cat's bed
my brother's friend
your sister's school

2 **We don't usually say** ~~the room of Dad, the car of John~~, **etc.**

Possessive adjectives

1 **We use possessive adjectives before a noun to say who something belongs to.**

My name's Joanne.
Is this your pen?
He's my brother. I'm his sister.
She's nice. I like her smile!
The cat isn't on its bed.
We love our house.
Are the students in their classroom?

2 **The possessive adjectives are:**

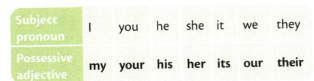

Subject pronoun	I	you	he	she	it	we	they
Possessive adjective	my	your	his	her	its	our	their

this / that / these / those

1 **We use this or these to point out things that are close to us. We use that or those to point out things that are not close to us or are close to other people.**

Look at this photograph – it's my sister.
These oranges aren't very nice.
That store is a really good place for clothes.
We don't like those boys.

2 **We use this or that with a singular noun. We use these or those with plural nouns.**

this photo	*that house*
these rooms	*those tables*

UNIT 4

there is / there are

1 *there is* (*there's*) **and** *there are* **are used to say that something exists.**

There's a small store on our street.
There are two supermarkets near here.
There are lots of great stores on Main Street.

2 *there's* **is the short form of** *there is*. **In speaking and informal writing, we usually say** *there's*.

3 **In positive sentences, we use** *there's* **with a singular noun and** *there are* **with plural nouns.**

There's a cat in the tree.
There's an old lady in the café.
There are nice stores on this street.

4 **In questions and negative sentences, we use** *a/an* **with a singular noun and** *any* **with plural nouns.**

Is there a bank near here?   *There isn't a bank near here.*
Are there any restaurants here?   *There aren't any restaurants here.*

some / any

1 **We use** *some* **and** *any* **with plural nouns.**

There are some good movies on TV tonight.
There aren't any games on my tablet.

2 **We use** *some* **in positive sentences. We use** *any* **in negative sentences and questions.**

There are some nice trees in the park.
There aren't any places to play soccer here.
Are there any good shoe stores in town?

Imperatives

1 **We use the imperative to tell someone to do something or not to do something.**

Come here!
Don't open the door!

2 **The positive imperative is the same as the base form of the verb.**

Turn right.
Open the window, please.

3 **The negative imperative is formed with** *Don't* **and the base form of the verb.**

Don't listen to him – he's wrong!
Don't open the window – it's cold in here.

UNIT 5
Simple present

1   The simple present is used to talk about things that happen regularly or are usually true.

   *I **go** to school at 8 o'clock every day.*
   *She **watches** TV after school.*
   *We **play** the piano.*
   *They **love** chocolate.*

2   The simple present is usually the same as the base form, but we add -s with third person singular (*he/she/it*).

   *I **like** pizza.*   *He **likes** pizza.*
   *They **live** in London.*   *She **lives** in London.*

3   If the verb ends with o, sh, ch, ss, z, or x, we add -es.

   *go – he go**es***   *finish – it finish**es***   *catch – she catch**es***
   *miss – it miss**es***   *fix – he fix**es***

4   If the verb ends with a consonant + -y, the y changes to i and we add -es.

   *carry – it carr**ies***   *study – he stud**ies***   *fly – it fl**ies***

5   If the verb ends with a vowel + -y, it is regular.

   *buy – she buy**s***   *say – he say**s***

Adverbs of frequency

1   Adverbs of frequency tell us *how often* people do things. Adverbs of frequency include:

   always   usually   often   sometimes   hardly ever   never

   100%   **0%**

2   Adverbs of frequency come after the verb *be*, but before other verbs.

   *I'm **always** hungry in the morning.*
   *I **usually** have breakfast at 7:00.*
   *He's **often** tired.*   *He **sometimes** goes to bed early.*
   *They're **never** late.*   *They **hardly ever** go on vacation.*

Simple present (negative)

The simple present negative is formed with *don't* (*do not*) or *doesn't* (*does not*) + base form of the verb.

*I **don't play** tennis.*
*She **doesn't play** soccer.*
*My grandparents **don't live** with us.*
*My brother **doesn't live** with us.*

Simple present (questions)

Simple present questions are formed with *Do / Does* + subject + base form of the verb.

Do you like the movie?   *Does Mike like shopping?*
Do I know you?   *Does she know the answer?*
Do your friends play video games?   *Does your dog play with a ball?*

UNIT 6
have / has (positive and negative)

1   The verb *have / has* is used to talk about things that people own.

   *I **have** a bicycle. (= There is a bicycle, and it is my bicycle.)*
   *He **has** a problem. (= There is a problem, and it is his problem.)*

2   We use *have* with *I/you/we/they*. We use *has* with *he/she/it*.

   *My mother **has** black hair and blue eyes.*
   *My friends **have** a nice cat.*
   *We **have** two fridges in our kitchen.*

3   The negative form is *don't / doesn't have*. We use *don't* with *I/you/we/they*. We use *doesn't* with *he/she/it*. We use *have* for all forms after *don't / doesn't*.

   *I **don't have** a tablet.*
   *This town **doesn't have** a park.*
   *They **don't have** a car.*

have / has (questions)

We make questions with *Do / Does* + subject + *have*. Short answers use *do / does* or *don't / doesn't*. Remember that we don't use *has* after *Do / Does*. (e.g., NOT: *Does he ~~has~~...?*)

Do you have my book?   *Yes, I **do**.*
Does your father have brown hair?   *Yes, he **does**.*
Does the store have any new games?   *No, it **doesn't**.*

Countable and uncountable nouns

Nouns in English are countable or uncountable.

1   Countable nouns have a singular and a plural form. We can count them. We use *a/an* with the singular nouns. We can use *some* with the plural nouns.

   *He has **a** house.*   *He has **two** houses.*
   *There's **a** picture on my wall.*   *There are **six** pictures on my wall.*
   *There's **an** orange in the fridge.*   *There are **some** oranges in the fridge.*

2   Uncountable nouns are always singular – they don't have a plural form. We can't count them. We can use *some* with uncountable nouns.

   *I like **music**.*   *Let's listen to **some** music.*
   *I like Japanese **food**.*   *Let's eat **some** Japanese **food**.*

3   We don't use *a/an* or numbers with uncountable nouns.

   NOT: *~~a bread~~*   *~~an information~~*   *~~three works~~*

UNIT 7
can (ability)

1 We use *can / can't* to talk about ability.

*I **can** swim.*
*I **can't** drive a car.*
*He **can** play the guitar.*
*He **can't** sing.*

2 The form is *can / can't* + the base form of the verb. To make questions, we use *Can* + subject + the base form of the verb. (We don't use *do / does* with *can* in questions or negative forms.)

*It's very small – I **can't read** it. (NOT: I don't can read it.)*
__Can you play__ this game? (NOT: Do you can play this game?)

3 Short answers are *Yes, … can* or *No, … can't*.

*Can he swim? **Yes, he can.***
*Can you sing? **No, I can't.***

Prepositions of time

We use different prepositions to talk about time.

1 With times of the day, we use *at*.

*School starts **at** 8 o'clock.*
*The train leaves **at** seven thirty.*

2 With months and seasons, we use *in*.

*It always rains **in** December.*
*We play soccer **in** the winter.*

3 With days of the week, we use *on*.

*I go to the movies **on** Saturday.*
*There's a test at school **on** Monday.*

UNIT 8
Present continuous

1 We use the present continuous to talk about things that are happening at the moment of speaking.

*Please be quiet – I**'m watching** a movie.*
*They're in the dining room – they**'re having** dinner.*
*Dad's in his office, but he **isn't working**.*
*Hey, Alex – **are** you **listening** to me?*

2 We form the present continuous with the simple present of *be* + the *-ing* form of the main verb. Questions and negatives are formed with the question/negative form of *be* + the *-ing* form of the main verb.

*I**'m watching** a movie, but I**'m not enjoying** it.*
*They**'re playing** soccer, but they **aren't playing** well.*
***Are** you **having** a good time? Yes, we **are**.*
***Is** she **doing** her homework? No, she **isn't**.*

3 If the verb ends in *-e*, we omit the *e* before adding *-ing*. If the verb ends in a consonant + vowel + consonant, we double the consonant before adding *-ing*.

leave   *We're **leaving** now.*
get   *It's **getting** dark – let's go home.*

like / don't like + -ing

When we use the verbs (*don't*) *like, love, hate,* and another verb, we usually use the *-ing* form of the other verb.

*We **love living** here.*
*I **like dancing** at parties.*
*She **doesn't like listening** to classical music.*
*They **hate going** to the movies.*

UNIT 9
must / mustn't

We use *must* / *mustn't* to talk about rules.

1 We use *must* to say that it's necessary to do something.

   We **must leave** now.
   You **must go** to the doctor.

2 We use *mustn't* to say that it's necessary not to do something.

   You **mustn't tell** other people.
   We **mustn't be** late.

3 The form is *must* / *mustn't* + the base form of the verb. We don't use *do* / *does* in negative sentences.

   You must **ask** me first.
   I mustn't **eat** a lot of snacks before dinner.
   (NOT: ~~I don't must eat a lot of snacks before dinner.~~)

can (asking for permission)

1 We often use *Can I* + verb to ask for permission (ask if it's OK) to do something.

   Can I ask a question, please?
   Can I watch the game on TV now?

2 We use *can* or *can't* to give or refuse permission.

   Can I use your phone?   Yes, you **can**.
                                 No, sorry, you **can't**. I'm using it.

I'd like … / Would you like …?

1 We use *would* ('d) + *like* to ask for something, or to offer something, in a nice way. It is more polite than *want*.

   I'd like a sandwich, please.
   Would you like a dessert?

2 *I'd like* is the short form of *I would like*. We almost always use it in speaking and informal writing.

UNIT 10
Simple past: *was / wasn't; were / weren't; there was / were*

1 We use the simple past form of *to be* to talk about actions and events in the past.

   It **was** a lovely day yesterday.
   They **were** at school last Friday.

2 We form the simple past of *be* like this:

singular	plural
I **was**	we **were**
you **were**	you **were**
he/she/it **was**	they **were**

3 We form the negative by adding *not* (*was not, were not*). In speaking and informal writing, we almost always use the short forms *wasn't* and *weren't*.

   I **wasn't** at home last night.
   She **wasn't** at the party.
   You **weren't** very happy yesterday.
   They **weren't** with us at the concert.

4 The simple past of *there is(n't)* / *there are(n't)* is *there was(n't)* / *there were(n't)*.

   There was a lot of rain yesterday.
   There weren't any interesting shows on TV last night.

Simple past: *Was he …? / Were you …?*

We form questions by putting the verb before the subject.

Were you late on Monday morning?
Was she at the movies with you?

Simple past: regular verbs

1 We use the simple past to talk about actions and events in the past.

   I **played** video games yesterday.
   They **liked** the movie on Friday.

2 With regular verbs, we form the simple past by adding *-ed*. It is the same for all subjects.

   He **closed** the window.
   The movie **finished** after midnight.
   You **called** me three times last night.
   We **wanted** to see them.

3 When the verb ends in *-e*, we only add *-d*. When the verb ends in consonant + *-y*, we change the *y* to *i* and then we add *-ed*.

   We **loved** the concert on Sunday.
   They **studied** for a long time before the test.

UNIT 11
Simple past: irregular verbs

1   Many English verbs are irregular. This means that the simple past forms are different – they don't have the usual -ed ending. For example:

go – **went**
make – **made**
give – **gave**
take – **took**
put – **put**

2   For every irregular verb, you need to remember the simple past form. There is a list of irregular verbs on page 128.

Simple past (negative)

We form negatives in the simple past with *didn't* (*did not*) and the base form of the verb. It's the same for both regular and irregular verbs. It's the same for all subjects.

talk	I **didn't talk**.
like	You **didn't like** it.
give	She **didn't give** me a present.
go	He **didn't go** to town.
take	We **didn't take** any photos.
make	They **didn't make** any money.

Simple past (questions)

We form questions in the simple past with *Did* + subject + the base form of the verb. It's the same for all verbs (regular and irregular) and for all subjects.

see	**Did** I **see** you in town on Saturday?
do	**Did** you **do** the homework last night?
go	**Did** your brother **go** to the same school?
take	**Did** they **take** you to the movies?

could / couldn't (ability)

To talk about ability in the past, we use *could/ couldn't* + the base form of a verb.

When I was small, I **could walk** on my hands.
We went to New York, but we **couldn't go** to the Statue of Liberty because it was closed.

UNIT 12
Comparative adjectives

1   We use the comparative form of the adjective + *than* to compare two things.

My sister is **younger than** me.
Australia is **smaller than** Brazil.
My new smartphone is **better than** the old one.

2   With short adjectives, we normally add -er.

new – new**er**
quiet – quiet**er**

With adjectives that end in -e, we just add -r.

nice – nice**r**
fine – fine**r**

With adjectives of two syllables that end with consonant + -y, we change the y to i and add -er.

easy – eas**ier**
healthy – health**ier**

With adjectives that end in consonant + vowel + consonant, we double the final consonant and add -er.

big – bi**gger**
hot – ho**tter**

3   With longer adjectives (i.e., with two or more syllables), we don't change the adjective – we put *more* in front of it.

expensive – **more expensive**
dangerous – **more dangerous**

4   Some adjectives are irregular – this means they have a different comparative form.

good – **better**
bad – **worse**
far – **further**

one / ones

1   Sometimes we don't want to repeat a noun. We can use *one* or *ones* in order not to repeat it.

The pizza was delicious – I want another (pizza) **one**.
These shoes are very expensive – I want cheaper (shoes) **ones**.

2   We use *one* to replace a singular noun and *ones* to replace a plural noun.

This red shirt is OK, but the blue **one** is nicer. (one replaces shirt)
I don't want to play these old games – let's buy some new **ones**. (ones replaces games)

IRREGULAR VERBS

Base form	Simple past
be	was/were
begin	began
buy	bought
can	could
catch	caught
choose	chose
come	came
do	did
draw	drew
drink	drank
drive	drove
eat	ate
fall	fell
feel	felt
find	found
fly	flew
get	got
give	gave
go	went
have	had
hear	heard
keep	kept
know	knew
learn	learned
leave	left

Base form	Simple past
light	lit
make	made
meet	met
pay	paid
put	put
read /riːd/	read /red/
ride	rode
run	ran
say	said
see	saw
send	sent
sing	sang
sit	sat
sleep	slept
speak	spoke
stand	stood
take	took
teach	taught
tell	told
think	thought
understand	understood
wake	woke
wear	wore
write	wrote